Facing Myself

Facing Myself

Reflections from Past Lives, Dreams, and Psychic Readings

by Jennifer Borchers

A.R.E. Press • Virginia Beach • Virginia

1st Printing, April 1994

Printed in the U.S.A.

A.R.E. Press
Sixty-Eighth & Atlantic Avenue
P.O. Box 656
Virginia Beach, VA 23451-0656

Library of Congress Cataloging-in-Publication Data
Borchers, Jennifer, 1943-
Facing myself: reflections from past lives, dreams, and psychic readings / by Jennifer Borchers.
p. cm.
Includes bibliographical references.
ISBN 0-87604-323-6
1. Borchers, Jennifer, 1943- . 2. Spiritual healing—Case studies. 3. Reincarnation therapy—Case studies. 4. New Age persons—Biography. I. Title.
BP605.N48B66 1994
133.8'092-dc29
[B] 94-288

Cover design by Patti McCambridge

Dedication

I dedicate this book to my anchors on this planet who have accepted and loved me into life: my mother, Sophie Meyer Borchers; my father, Johann Dietrich Borchers; my grandmother, Katharina Schniedewind Borchers; my grandfather, Heinrich Borchers; my brothers, Heinz, Bernhard, Richard, and Johann Borchers; my sisters, Catharina Borchers Bianco, Bertha Borchers von Hassel, Hanni Borchers Fick, and Tina Borchers Gould. All my relationships with them are precious gifts. The many birthdays, weddings, confirmations, showers, anniversaries, reunions, and other holidays I have celebrated with them are impressed on my soul, and I hope to take the memories with me into future lives.

I gratefully acknowledge the love, friendship, and support I have received throughout my life from Christa Hinck Cordes, Rosemarie Kinder Voltz, Monika Wildeboer Kroos, Helga Pfeifer, Sigrid Vogt Bense, John Brademas, John Mroz, Shona Brogden Stirbl, James Keogh, Wieland Flecken, Kevin Trainor, Martin Sinclair, Ron Carozzoni, Anne Stenson, Betty Zevallo, Renee Moder, Anne Pellegrim, Edan Schappert, and Sylvia Leonard.

Table of Contents

Preface

WHEN I was twelve years old, my brown hair was plaited into two thick braids, and I wore a faded dress my older sisters had worn before me. I stood next to my mother on a Sunday morning in the 300-year-old Lutheran church in a small village in north Germany and sang hymn number 188 that was based on the 103rd Psalm. As a candidate for confirmation, I was required to attend church every two weeks. The words and melody filled me with infinite sweetness, immeasurable sadness, and a tiny ray of hope, "Praise, my soul, the Lord, what is within me, and His holy name." I felt good singing God's praises because music made sweetness flow through my blood. But why should I praise Him? The woman beside me, my mother, had held me hostage since the day of my birth. When she was not ignoring me, she was yelling at me, reminding me that she could take my life any time she pleased. Living in silent fear of her every day, I did whatever chores she demanded of me. Because she disapproved of my showing my feelings, I hid them deep inside me.

The song we were singing that day continued, "As for man, his days are as grass; as a flower of the field, so he flourisheth. For the wind passeth over it, and it is gone; and the place thereof shall know it no more." I saw my days as grass and myself as a flower. Was I a tiny purple violet, seen by no one, yet humbly living my life, praising the Lord? Or was I a great big golden sunflower, standing tall and bringing pleasure to those who saw me? I felt like an insignificant violet that would have liked to be a glorious sunflower. Like the grass and like the flowers, I would soon be gone, too. The wind would blow me away like a speck of dust, and that was well for then my suffering would be over.

But years have passed, and the wind has not blown me away. In 1961, at the age of seventeen, I emigrated to the United States. I have been economically self-supporting ever since, working as housekeeper, delicatessen clerk, stenographer, secretary, and executive secretary in New York City. I obtained a bachelor's degree from New York University in 1986 and a master's degree from the City University of New York in 1992. Recently I exuberantly celebrated my fiftieth birthday.

Physically, I was blessed with excellent health from the start. Emotionally and mentally I faced many challenges. At first, I suffered in silence. Around the age of thirty, however, my emotional and mental pain was so great that I considered suicide. I realized that I had a choice. I could either become the wind and blow my own life away, or I could break out of my silent suffering and ask for professional help. I did not trust authority figures, such as conventional therapists, but if they failed to help me, I resolved, I could still end my life. Five years of therapy, however, from 1975 to 1980, opened me to new possibilities. I began a fascinating journey into inner space and finally came to understand my own feelings and thoughts.

For the ten years preceding therapy, I had studied the theories of metaphysical teachers, among them Edgar Cayce and Alice Bailey. Partially, I had used these theories as an escape from my real-life problems. On the other hand, they had fed me spiritually and helped keep me alive. As I came down to earth and took a firmer hold of my physical body, some unexpected, but marvelous things happened to me.

In 1972, I experienced a series of partial astral projections that culminated in one exquisite out-of-body experience in full consciousness from beginning to end. I experienced my body, mind, and soul as three interconnected aspects of one whole. These astral projections were the first concrete evidence to me that the metaphysical theories were true. The discovery that the knowledge contained in the books was verifiable by experience and that I could do it myself without the aid of experts was enormously exciting and empowering.

Once I had firmly decided to live, I looked at my emotional and mental problems, or *challenges*, as Edgar Cayce called them. My mother's abuse had left deep scars in my psyche, and I still expected to be abused every day at every turn; her neglect had taught me to neglect myself. My father's gentleness and fear of pain, on the other hand, had taught me to deny my own pain. I was afraid of people, did not trust anyone, resented everyone, and did not reveal myself to others. I had neither personal will nor identity, and I was estranged from my feelings and desires. With the help of a therapist, I began my healing process. I had learned from spiritual healers that forgiveness is an absolute necessity to emotional and mental healing, and so I taught myself to forgive my parents and, eventually, myself.

While mentally engaged in recalling childhood experiences to discuss in therapy sessions, to my utter surprise I experienced a vivid vision in full waking consciousness of a past-life time when I was a member of the Incan society in Peru before Europeans arrived in the Americas. I saw myself as a young maiden who, as the most virtuous and talented, was chosen to be sacrificed to invoke blessings from the Sun God. I was shocked by the vision and the idea that I, feeling troubled and insignificant, was blessed with an awesome vision that convinced me beyond a reasonable doubt that my everyday reality was only a narrow facet of a much larger reality. However, just as I had felt set apart earlier by the abuse I had suffered, now I felt set apart by experiences which I could not readily share without the risk of being thought weird.

The solution to this dilemma was a closer relationship with the inner divinity, the indwelling God, which Edgar Cayce called the "still small voice within." I still saw God as a punishing Being who lay in wait to catch me committing sins for which He would then promptly punish me. My membership in spiritual organizations, attending spiritual workshops, the unusual experiences I had, meditation, and prayer eventually enabled me to heal my fear and distrust of God and establish a close and loving relationship with a wise and loving God. The indwelling Divine, God within, is now a living reality to me upon whom I trust and depend.

Although I had struggled with deep-seated despair for many years, I never suffered from loneliness. I have kept friends from as far back as grammar school days and make new friends easily. I am blessed with many members of my extended family who live here in the United States, including four sisters and two brothers in New York State, eighteen nieces and nephews, eight great-nephews and one great-niece. In the romance department, however, I tended to become too easily attached and detached. At this stage in my life, I have not yet formed a lasting marital relationship.

In retrospect, I am grateful for everything that has happened to me. I consider my emotional and intuitive sensitivity a precious gift that I need to take good care of and use properly. Years of existing and feeling more like an object than a human being have given way to living while in touch with my feelings, my wishes, and my creativity.

The years of sorrow and confusion are over, and my life has finally become full of delights and adventures. I treasure the out-of-body experiences, the dreams, the many glimpses of past lives, psychic readings, my relationship with my soul, and my relationships with my friends, colleagues, and members of my extended family. This book describes half a century of my life, my journey of facing myself while traveling from darkness into light. My wish is that my story may strengthen and inspire all those who read it.

Jennifer Borchers

Chapter 1
Into the Body, into the World

There was a child went forth every day,
And the first object he look'd upon, that object he became,
And that object became part of him for the day or a certain
  part of the day,
Or for many years or stretching cycles of years.
—(From: *There Was a Child Went Forth*, by Walt Whitman)

THE early morning of November 22, 1943, was cold and damp in the village of Köhlen in northern Germany. All the healthy men had been inducted into Hitler's army, including my father. At six o'clock, my thirty-three-year-old mother, Sophie, arose out of her warm feather bed in an unheated room. In her nightgown, she left her bedroom and walked through the children's room and saw her four young ones, ages nine, seven, five, and three asleep in their beds. She went to the kitchen to make a fire, but her body ached as it had ached four times before and would ache four more times in the years to come. She lit the fire but did not get dressed to milk the cows. Instead, she went to my grandparents' bedroom and woke my grandmother. She said to her, "I am not going to milk the cows today. The child is coming. I am going back to bed."

There was no doctor in the village, and the midwife lived several miles away. The women in the neighborhood were mothers and had experience helping other women give birth. My grandmother said, "Yes, go back to bed. I will go and get a neighbor to help."

Many years later when visiting her in Germany, my mother told me about these events on the morning of my birth. When Grandmother returned, I had already been born, and Mother had considered Grandmother as useless. She said disparagingly, "The *girl* is already born." She also had contempt for the girl she had just given birth to, having hoped for a second boy. She had thus far birthed one son, and then three daughters in a row, and now me.

She also told me that during the war when I was a baby, whenever Allied planes flew overhead, everyone was afraid of being hit by a bomb. She took her five children and fled into the fields, a mile or two beyond the houses. The road leading to the fields was of dirt and could get very muddy in the summer. Since I was too small to walk and the baby carriage could not be maneuvered along the dirt road, I was pushed along in a wheelbarrow by my ten-year-old brother, Heinz. Usually my mother headed for a sand pit at the foot of our fields and a grove of birch trees surrounded by blooming patches of August heather, where we hid out until the sky was quiet. Then, after the planes had passed, we would trek back to the farm.

Another story she told me reveals my incredible good luck during a bombing. My mother, grandmother, and a relative from Bremerhaven who had come to live with us to escape the bombing of the city had labored all morning in the front yard grating a sack of potatoes to make flour for baking bread. There were five children to feed and all the rye flour had been picked up by Hitler's soldiers. The women put the potato mixture into a big zinc washtub to settle before they would pour off the water and let the flour dry.

Suddenly there was a tremendous blast. Dust whirled up. Windows shattered in the houses nearby. Intended for the sawmill a hundred yards away, the bomb fell on our neighbor's rye field across the road, just missing the sawmill. The dust ruined the potato flour. The women, upset and wailing, almost distracted my mother from remembering that she had left me in the open baby carriage directly under the window in her bedroom. What had the glass done to her baby? She rushed into the house and into her room. Both shocked and relieved, she discovered not a scratch nor cut on my face and arms, even though the pillow that covered me was completely filled with glass shards from the blasted window.

I spent the first year of my life in a large wicker bassinet on the dresser in my parents' bedroom. My mother picked me up when I was hungry and breast-fed me for twelve months. She was fastidious in changing my diapers and bathing me regularly. Taking care of five children under the age of ten, plus the farm work during the war, must have been a difficult assignment. My father, Johann, was a soldier for the first eighteen months of my life. My mother did not know that infants need attention to develop emotionally and mentally, and beyond taking care of my physical needs, she paid no attention to me. She told me later that I cried frequently as an infant and slept little. She told me that when she had to make a bike trip into the village, she would leave the house only after she had lulled me to sleep. When she returned half an hour later and looked in on me, invariably I would be lying there awake, with my eyes wide open.

I have a vague memory of frequently feeling cold while in the bassinet, especially around my shoulders. Winters in north Germany were very cold, and the bedroom was unheated. As soon as a fire was lit in the kitchen and living room, the bassinet would be moved to a warmer room. Chances are I spent many mornings and afternoons in the living room while my grandfather read, my grandmother knitted, and both kept an eye on me.

My brother Bernhard was born when I was two-and-a-half years old. A family snapshot taken that summer in front of the farmhouse shows my parents, grandparents, Heinz, and my sister Catharina in the back row. I stand in front between my other sisters Hanni and Bertha. My chin-length hair, which later would turn the color of chestnuts, was still blond. It hung loosely down, except for the top strand which was gathered with a comb. I wore brown leather over-the-ankle shoes, apparently without socks. What attracts my attention in the photograph are my hands, which I held in two tight fists on either side.

Around the time of my brother's birth, when I was two-and-a-half, my mother told me point blank, "I'm not going to take care of you any more; take care of yourself." Perhaps she was only half serious, but I remember the emotional shock and feeling like being kicked out of the nest. An image is connected to this time around my brother's birth. In this memory I see myself, a little girl wearing clumsy over-the-ankle shoes without socks, standing alone and forgotten in the big hall in the farmhouse. A moment ago the space around me was filled with adults, my mother, grandmother, and my father. They were busily moving about and talking. But suddenly they were gone, and I was all alone. I was shocked. I did not comprehend what had happened. I experienced, I seemed to actually see, the energy fields of the adults separating from me and moving away through doors that opened and swallowed them up. I remained standing motionless in the middle of a vast empty space, a helpless, unwanted child, dependent on adults who did not want to be depended on.

My mother, of course, continued to take care of my physical needs, fed, clothed, washed me, and daily combed my hair into two braids. But emotionally she abandoned me in favor of my brother. During the next year or two I began to fear her for the threatening and accusing words she said to me, often when she and I were alone in the kitchen and there were no witnesses. The older children would be in school, my father out working in the fields, and my grandparents would be in the living room. She would run hurriedly to and fro, ignoring my presence as if I were an unnecessary object. When she noticed me, she was usually in a state of frustration, despair, and anger, and I became her scapegoat. She would verbally attack my innocence, sanity, goodness, worth, and importance as a human being, especially because I was female.

For this, the district's religion, Lutheranism, with its belief in original sin, gave her much ammunition. When she felt at her lowest, she would attack my right to be alive with actual threats of death and dismemberment. Her threats terrified me to the point of my being afraid of being alone in a room with her. My terror of physical violence was heightened by a mental image that, at the time, I thought was an expression of my fear of her. I saw myself lying on the ground, beaten and dying, while uncaring people stepped over my body.

When I was a child, I did not know that I was emotionally more sensitive than my brothers and sisters. They might laugh off Mother's cruelties or know that she would not act on her threats, but I recoiled in horror and fear at the negative and harmful energy that emanated from her. The words that came out of her mouth hit me like glass shards, like razor blades, and cut me to the quick. Psychic pain was not a reality to her, and showing my pain resulted not in an apology and compassion, but in ridicule. The way to survive, I learned, was by hiding my hurt and denying that she had any affect on me.

Showing love and affection was not part of the north German culture, and my mother showed little affection to any of her children. She took literally the old adage, "Children should be seen but not heard." She must have verbalized this to me and my sisters and brothers dozens of times. She enforced strict discipline with threats and insults. Occasionally, when Bernhard and I played livelier than pleased her, she would yell at us: "I could take one of you and use him as a weapon to kill the other one." She yelled at me many times that she would like to kill me or that it would be cheaper to kill me than to raise me. She would follow up a threat of death with an insult that underscored my unimportance, "When you are dead, not even the cock will crow." She seldom used physical punishment, but it was unnecessary because I was so terrified of her that I did whatever she demanded of me.

She herself felt overwhelmed and was terrified of the needs of her children. Expressing a need or even a preference resulted in ridicule from her. Somehow, I received the message that if I would take care of her first, she would then take care of me. I was sensitive, perceptive, needy, hopeful, and trusting, and so I took care of her needs while I hoped and waited for her to recognize that I had needs also. But she chose not to see my needs.

Many years later she told me proudly how she had taught her children early to fend for themselves and not to depend on her—as early as infancy. "When you were in the bassinet and you threw your toy on the floor and expected me to get it back for you," she told me, "I took you and held you upside down and made you pick it up yourself. You learned fast not to throw it out again."

"You did this only to me?" I asked, alarmed.

"No, to all you children," she replied.

From the time I was small, my mother prevented me from expressing myself in her presence. On a feeling level, it was as if whenever I as much as moved or thought of saying something, she would aim aggressive energy at me to stop me. I was sensitive to her feelings; on a deep level her negativity revolted me, and I did not like to touch her. If she was at all sensitive to my psychic reactions, they did not help to make her love me.

If it rained at the wrong time or the chickens did not lay enough eggs, she would point at someone and say, "It's your fault." I was often the one she singled out for blame. Accusation was also her way of dealing with my need for comfort and support. If I dared to come to her after being hurt by another child, her response was, "It's your own fault." Any kind of mishap that occurred to me—if a favorite pencil broke or I wore a hole in a favorite pair of shoes—her response was, "It's your own fault." I grew up feeling guilty for things I had no control over.

I was intimidated by her angry injunctions that were phrased as innocent questions: Can't you do anything right? What is wrong with you? Aren't you ashamed of yourself? Have you gone completely mad? She never said there was something wrong with me or that I was mad, but that is how I felt.

Our house stood in the country in a cluster of homes a mile from the village, and I was able to find much solace and comfort in nature. I loved to walk through the family vegetable garden which my grandmother kept. There were large beds of peas so tall that anyone could easily hide behind them. In back was a row of gooseberry and lingonberry bushes. I loved to crouch there on the moist, rich soil, the evergreen hedge behind me, the berry bushes before me, and munch the juicy tart berries and feel safe.

In back of the farmhouse was an apple orchard. The bushy hedge behind it was two yards wide and offered many beautiful hiding places where anyone could pick handfuls of dainty anemones. I brought bouquets of wild flowers to my mother, in a desperate attempt to win her love, but she did not honor my gifts. I would often find the flowers carelessly tossed on the bench behind the table, already wilted.

Anyone who approached our house on the dirt road that led from the main road would first see the vegetable garden to the left and then the old barn. The front courtyard between the barn and the main house was paved with cobblestones. Next to the road and to the right of the courtyard stood a clump of strong, healthy oak and beech trees. These trees were our lightning rods as they towered well above the house.

The house was an old-fashioned German Fachwerkhaus, built by my grandfather, Heinrich, in 1904, the year before his marriage to my grandmother, Katharina. The roof, originally thatched, was later replaced with tiles. The living quarters for the family were in the rear of the house; the front part housed our milch cows and several calves during winters, but was empty in summers. The large front hall had a cement floor and a wooden ceiling. The attic was one huge room and was used to store about twenty-five loads of hay at one end and an equal number of straw at the other. This was fodder for the animals in winter.

My mother raised poultry, guinea hens, turkeys, and geese and sold them at Christmas time. She also earned money with lace making, called tatting, which she did primarily during long winter evenings in the living room. As she worked, she and my father would sit on the couch, with maybe one child between them, while Grandfather sat in the chair by the stove and Grandmother on the opposite end. My brothers and sisters would spread out around the table, doing their homework. Sometimes the most beautiful flowers, amaryllis, birds of paradise, bloomed on the window sill in our living room. My mother had bartered farm produce for them from the wife of the gardener, with whom she had a friendly relationship.

My mother's other talent was baking. She and Grandmother had always baked breads and butter cakes in a free-standing brick oven located in the farmyard. It was heated twice a month, and neighbors were invited to bake their breads with us. In 1958, my brother Heinz and sister Catharina in the U.S. sent money for Mother to buy an electric oven and stove. The oven came with a cookbook and a baking book, and for the next three years my mother tried out a new baking recipe every Saturday afternoon. Marble cake with lemon icing, eclairs, two-layer apple cake with frosting, three-layer tortes, butter cake. At Christmas time she filled several fifteen-liter milk cans with white and brown spice cookies, and we children could eat as many as we wanted. When she baked, there was no selfishness, no resentment, no begrudging. Her love of baking was obvious, as was her love to share the baked goods with the family. The only times I felt loved by my mother was when I watched her bake and especially when she invited me to eat what she had created with a "Come on, it's ready, have a piece!"

Before my birth, my father was called to serve in Hitler's army and obeyed the call since refusing would have meant certain death by firing squad. My mother said that the war had changed him in that he resigned his personal will and whatever little aggressiveness he had possessed earlier. He returned from the war with physical injuries in his left hand and right shoulder. The shot through his left shoulder actually saved his life. He received it in the Crimea on the way to the Russian front from where few German soldiers returned alive. He never talked about the war or what he experienced then. He never set foot in a church again either, but found divinity in nature and expressed it in simple and gentle living.

My father was 5'8" and of slight build. He combed his jet-black hair straight back over his head. He had an older brother, two older and one younger sisters. All four had emigrated to the U.S. during the '20s and '30s because their mother, Katharina, had talked so much about New York after spending four years there before marrying my grandfather, Heinrich. Heinrich forbade my father to emigrate, insisting that he take over the farm. My father had the gentleness of a poet and artist rather than the toughness of a farmer. I loved my father, but for most of my childhood I thought he was a weak man, perhaps because he was nonaggressive and because he did not protect me from my mother and denied that her power, which to me was cruel and brought me constant pain, even existed.

In my first visual memory of him, I was in the farmyard in the late afternoon in the summer. I expected him to come home for dinner from working in the fields. As soon as I saw him coming down the dirt road on his bicycle, I ran as fast as my little legs let me. I met him about 100 yards from the house. He smiled at me, stopped the bike, picked me up, and set me down on the metal bar in front of him. He sat down on the saddle and continued pedaling in a slow and steady rhythm right up to the front door. I jumped off, feeling very happy and ran away to play.

My father humbly loved all little creatures, especially his many children. He loved us in quiet ways and showed his love without making a display of it. Every spring he carried out two predictable acts of love for us. First, as soon as the sun had warmed the earth after the long winter, he would hitch the team of oxen to the wagon and make two trips that had nothing to do with farm work. He would drive to a sand pit among the fields about a mile and a half away and come back with a load of the cleanest, whitest sand imaginable. He would then unload it underneath the two beech trees in the front yard where we children would have a sand pile to play in, while our mother kept an eye on us.

His second act of love every spring was to fasten a strong chain to two hooks on a ceiling beam close to the front door inside the farmhouse and make a swing. A wooden board with two notches served as a seat. This swing was unique, and I never saw another one like it in any other farmhouse. It was also indestructible, yet he would insist on trying it out to make sure it was safe. I see him now, swinging back and forth with all his might, aiming to get his feet as far as possible out the front door and at the same time as high as possible. When he was satisfied or—as I see it now—when he had satisfied his own inner child's need to play, he took me or a brother or sister on his lap and gave us a ride, back and forth, in slow, smooth movements, teaching us at the same time to hold on tight and to swing with all our might.

I remember spending many long winter afternoons in the 1940s and '50s with him in his workshop, located in the barn, where he made wooden shoes by hand. He would cut the trees himself in the forest, saw them into the proper length, and bring them home on the oxen wagon. Not only did his family wear his handmade shoes, but relatives and people in the village requested them and paid money for them. He would measure his customers' feet and have them try them on for size before they were sold. I remember wearing them at home and to school during the fifties. They were lacquered black and had a piece of sheepskin on top so that the top of the wearer's foot was protected where the wood pressed on it. They were great fun to wear in the wintertime because the snow stuck to the soles, and I would become taller and taller and walked as if on stilts.

By the time I was six years old, Heinz was sixteen; Catharina, Bertha, and Hanni were fourteen, twelve, and ten years old, respectively; and my mother had given birth to Bernhard, Richard, and Tina, ages four, two, and a few months old. Five years later my youngest brother Johann would follow. I remember my first day of school in April

1950. Although I did not know it, my mother was pregnant with my younger sister who would be born in July. She would not take me to school, and I was disappointed. She had taken the others, and I would have liked to have her undivided attention on the walk there. It was arranged that Hella Stüve, a girl two years older who lived close by, would take me, since her class began at the same time as mine. My mother washed and dressed me, brushed my hair and braided it into pigtails. Then came the matter of which shoes I was to wear. Wooden shoes were O.K. later on, but not on a girl's first day in school, it was decided, probably by my grandmother.

I vividly remember sitting in a chair in the hall next to a mountain of shoes, nearly all of them sent by relatives in the States. My frustrated mother fit me with one pair after another while Hella looked on. None fit. My grandmother wrung her hands, "The girl has to go to school and has no shoes to wear. Why was this left for the last minute?" Why indeed? If my grandmother had been in charge, she would have seen to it during the week before. Why wasn't she in charge? I wondered why she wasn't my mother. I wished she were. Eventually a pair of shoes that fit were found, and off I went with Hella. That first day of school, and every school day thereafter, was heaven to me because my mother was not there, and I felt safe from her insults and threats. Fortunately I was a good student, although not right away. I spoke only *Plattdeutsch*, an ancient spoken form of German, and the teacher spoke *Hochdeutsch*, the language of books and the media. It took me less than a year to catch up.

I also had my first crush that year on a boy in my class. His name was Detlef. He and his family were fugitives from East Germany who had settled in our village. He was not earthy and simple like the local farm boys, but sensitive, gentle, and a dreamer. I remember him standing alone in an elevated corner in the schoolyard—sucking his thumb. I felt attracted to him and loved him deeply, but his family moved away before the first school year was over.

When I received my first report card, I felt inordinately proud. It was not a particularly good report card. Actually, it was quite ordinary. But to me it was special, because it was about me and only about me. I didn't have to share it with any of my sisters. In addition, my teacher had written a personal note in it about me. Contrary to my mother, my teacher had noticed that I existed and thought that I was important enough to write about. The note said something to the effect that I was a quiet and orderly child, a bit too sensitive in socializing with the other children. Of course, my mother saw the word "sensitive" as criticism and used it against me to cause me pain. But I was so proud that my teacher had noticed my existence that the pleasure of that feeling insulated me from my mother's disapproving remarks. For as long as the report card remained in our house, I proudly showed it to any neighbor who visited us. To this day, the bottom of the card shows the smudgy print of my thumb where I tightly held it. I think I must have shown it several times to the mailman, whom I liked because he was friendly and noticed me.

In school I gained confidence and began to speak up at home. But my mother always judged my comments and statements as wrong or stupid and aggressively contradicted me. When I dared to make a negative remark about the behavior of a neighbor or a relative, she stopped me and demanded that my behavior be absolutely perfect. As long as I was imperfect, I had no right to notice anyone else's imperfection.

Many years later, after reading books by Alice Miller, the Swiss psychoanalyst, I understood that my mother acted out of fear that if I could perceive the goodness or badness of other people's behavior, I would also see what was right and wrong in her behavior, and this she wanted to prevent. The result was, however, that I did not learn to judge which people were harmful to me and which were good for me.

My grammar school class, made up of children born in the war year of 1943, was small, with four girls and eight boys. Two of the girls, Christa and Rosemarie, became my friends. The friendships, still active today, lasted through eight years of grammar school, the only schooling required at that time in Germany. I saw both women in 1987 on my last visit to Germany, and Christa visited me in New York in 1989 with one of her daughters and a niece.

In a geography lesson one day, our teacher talked about Columbus being the first man to travel to America in 1492 and discover the Native Americans, whom he called savages. This was the first time I heard about Native Americans. I had a curious reaction in my mind that said, "What is he talking about, 'discovered the Native Americans'? They have always been there. I always knew they were there. And who is he calling 'savages'? They were honorable and noble." My mind contained vague images of Native Americans living in vast expanses of land in complete harmony with nature.

When I was a child, I had a flair for language and poetry. When my sixth grade teacher, Herr Koop, assigned our class to memorize a poem with six verses, he said that he wanted everyone to learn the first four verses by heart, but only I was to learn also the final two. He said these verses were difficult to pronounce and only I could hope to do it correctly. In the final two verses the poet, Adelbert von Chamisso, compared his life with that of an old washerwoman he admired and expressed his hope that his death would be as meaningful as hers. Teacher Koop tutored me in the pronunciation and the pauses; mysteriously through the poetry I got in touch with something within me that, because Herr Koop valued it, I, too, began to see it as extraordinarily precious.

At home, my mother pounced on everything that came out of my mouth which came from *me*. She ridiculed me into feeling ashamed. What was this something within me that Herr Koop valued and that I could feel inside me, when I was immersed in the poetry, as something beautiful and precious? It wasn't just that I was smart. Somehow, it was connected to what was in the poetry—beauty, rhythm, harmony, and wisdom. If this were truly within me, it contradicted my mother's opinion that what was in me was inherently bad, stupid, uncivilized, and ugly. At the time, the beauty, rhythm, harmony, and wisdom felt as real to me and as much a part of me as did the badness, stupidity, and ugliness.

When I was nine, a family moved into the neighborhood with a girl my age, and because of her I learned several things. Birgit and her mother and stepfather were from a large city. Her father was the forest ranger for the community; her mother was a housewife. Birgit and I became friends. She was fascinated with me because I lived on a farm, and I was fascinated with her because she didn't. Her family stayed in the village for only two years, then moved to Bederkesa, ten kilometers away, but during the two years that we were friends she gave me several wonderful gifts without even knowing it. One time she and I left her room with me clutching her beautiful book of Grimm's fairy tales under my arm. Her mother did not want me to take it. Birgit angrily stamped her foot and said, "But it is *my* book! You told me I can do with my things as I want!"

"But it is such a beautiful book!" her mother protested. "And there are so many children in Jennifer's house. It may get damaged."

"She will take good care of it!"

I was amazed not only that Birgit expressed anger at her mother, but that her mother gave in and Birgit won the argument. In my house it was inconceivable that I or any of my brothers or sisters would express anger toward my mother or father. They would have instantly put us in a place of subservience by painfully shaming us.

Another time, Birgit and I entered her house to get something from her room. Her mother was in the living room, rummaging through a drawer, and she was openly crying. I had never seen my mother cry, so had believed that adults never cry. Not only that, but I believed that crying was a weakness, even for children. Here was a woman from the city, who was educated, pretty, with an easy, usually happy life, and she cried. It made me feel shy. I thought something was seriously wrong with her, but Birgit talked to her and said to me in a way that indicated this was nothing unusual, "She has a headache. She is looking for some aspirin."

Then she shrugged her shoulders. I thought that if such a woman can cry with no feeling of shame, then maybe it is all right to cry. Maybe, I thought, it is abnormal never to cry.

Another time Birgit and I had wandered around the fields and meadows for some time and crawled underneath the hedge at the far end of our orchard. While we were picking spring anemones, she told me casually that she liked me. Many years later in 1979, I began a poem called "Childhood" with that particular scene: //Birgit told me that she liked me that April // when I was nine // and she was new in town. // We crawled on our hands and knees, // Picked dainty anemones, white and yellow, // underneath high bushes . . . // It was the first time // anybody had ever told me that. //

When she told me, my first reaction was that she was wrong to tell me that she liked me and that she was weak. Maybe she wanted something from me? But then I remembered other times when she behaved in a way that caught my attention because it was different from what I was accustomed to. I thought that maybe her way was better than mine and of the village people who did not tell one another of their good feelings for each other. The village people delighted in showing off their indifference to others and sometimes rubbed in how unnecessary others were to their well-being and happiness. Being told by Birgit that she liked me made me feel good. I could not help but value that feeling in spite of the many verbal and nonverbal messages I had received that feeling something, anything, was weak. I admired Birgit for having the honesty to be true to her feelings and for the generosity she showed in sharing them with me. I felt that I had received a precious gift from her.

My mother liked Birgit, as she did Christa and Rosemarie, my other girl friends. The irony was that she seemed to like them more than she liked me. She would ask them how they were that day, and how was their mother, and how was the family? She never asked me how I was. She would rather strike me before asking me how I felt. I was supposed to feel what she told me to feel and be the way she wanted me to be. Whenever my friends came over, I felt the difference in my mother's attitude. It both hurt and puzzled me. I thought there was something wrong with me, that it was my fault my mother didn't like me, that I was as bad as she had so often told me.

The old washerwoman in the poem by von Chamisso reminded me of my paternal grandmother, whom I called Oma. She was a very special person in my life. Orphaned at the age of five, she was adopted by a Lutheran family and received much love. Consequently she had solid love and acceptance for herself as a woman. At the age of fifteen in 1899, she and her two older sisters traveled to the United States, and she spent four years working as a housekeeper and receptionist for a lawyer in New York City. She still remembered English and loved to speak it with visitors.

What set Oma most apart from my mother was that she showed me that she liked me. There was no doubt about that. When Oma was around, I felt almost as safe as when my father was around. I loved to be with Oma in the vegetable garden, in the orchard, or in her living room. One spring day, I must have been eight or nine, she sat on the bench in front of the house.

"Come, sit with me, talk with me," she said and gave me a broad inviting smile. I felt like an adult because of her explicit invitation and walked over and sat with her. She looked at me again with an open inviting smile, urging me to talk about something, but I was pitifully unable to initiate a conversation. Nothing worth saying came to my mind. At that moment, even though I was only eight or nine years old, I knew that my ability to converse had been damaged by my mother's neglect and her constant threats, criticisms, and condemnations of me. On top of that, I felt as if I had let my grandmother down by being unable to initiate a conversation, and I felt sad. But Oma loved me almost unconditionally, neither resenting nor blaming me for my inability to talk.

When I was about twelve years old, Oma took me to visit Hella who, like Birgit, had lived in the neighborhood but moved to Bederkesa. We had gone there to celebrate Hella's birthday. Hella was not really my friend as much as my sister Hanni's friend. I was surprised that Oma took me instead of Hanni, but I think Hanni was unable to go for some reason. I loved being alone with my grandmother on the bus. What I remember most about the visit is what happened after we arrived in this strange living room with a lot of strange people, adults and children. One by one these people, including my grandmother, stepped forward, congratulated Hella on her birthday, and gave her a present. I made several attempts to step forward and to open my mouth, but again and again someone else got ahead of me and I stood back. My grandmother noticed and encouraged me with a broad and accepting smile, completely free of criticism, as if she wanted to say, "I know you'll do it; you can do it now, or you can do it later. I'm with you whenever you do it." I was the last one to step forward and say my well-rehearsed line, feeling my grandmother's good will surrounding me.

For many years during my childhood I slept in one of the three beds in my grandparents' bedroom. Grandfather's bed stood at one end of the room. Grandma's and mine stood side by side, with a narrow aisle in between, at the other end by the window. My sister Tina usually shared my bed. One night I heard company in the living room. I picked out the voices of my parents, grandparents, and two neighbors. Grandma was the happiest and the most popular. I dropped off to sleep but woke up again when she came to bed. She was restless and turned from one side to the other several times. Suddenly she let out a moan and a cry:

"I am so alone. Oh God, I am so alone!"

I was shocked and frightened. How could the most popular person in the family feel lonely? How could the kindest and most loving person I knew feel such pain? I nearly held my breath, but within minutes Grandmother was asleep and breathing deeply and peacefully. I was awake for a long time because my twelve-year-old mind couldn't handle the paradox that exists between a person's public and private world. The next morning Grandma was as happy as ever. I dismissed the experience, but it stayed in my subconscious as a warning not to be satisfied with appearances, but to look for the deeper reality.

Today I know that I owe a lot to my grandmother: gentleness, compassion for others, and probably my sanity. During the 1980s psychoanalyst Alice Miller studied in depth the effects parents have on their children. In general, if a child is abused, that child as an adult will become like the abusive parent and abuse children in turn without understanding. But if an abused child has an adult in her life who loves her and models another reality, this child has a good chance of imitating the loving adult. That, I think, was the case with me.

There was a woman in our neighborhood, Frau Brandjen, who was a second grandmother to me for a while. She had unconditional good will toward me, and I was hopelessly devoted to her. When she talked to me, she was so gentle. Where my mother's words were like razor blades that cut me to the quick, Frau Brandjen's words were like candy that I ate up with my heart. But one day when I was about twelve, the relationship was spoiled through circumstances beyond my control. Frau Brandjen had asked me, as she had many times before, to bike into the village to the baker and to pick up her favorite cake, a delicate mocha layer cake, which she had ordered for the upcoming holiday.

I rode my mother's adult bike two kilometers into the village in a standing position, as I was too short to sit in the saddle and reach the pedals. Children's bikes were still unheard of in the village in the years after the war. Because of the holiday, the baker had run out of box tops and so gave me the delicate cake in only the bottom part of a flexible cardboard box. He did not even tie a string around it. I carefully put the open box with the cake on its rack in back of the saddle. Holding it with my right hand, I pushed and steered the bike with my left. It was a precarious journey, as I could not get a good grip on the cardboard box, and steering the bike with my left hand was difficult. Halfway home, the front wheel slipped off a large cobblestone, I lost control, and the bike, the box, and I crashed to the ground. Instantly the cake was in smithereens, and so was my heart. I sat beside the cake and wept the bitterest tears I had ever wept. I accepted full responsibility for smashing the cake and blamed myself as brutally as I had learned to do from my mother.

A man from the village rode by on his bike, stopped, and tried to console me. It was not my fault, he said. I was only a child and the baker had done a foolish thing in not wrapping the cake properly. The baker was wrong, he said, not me. But I did not listen to him. I only knew that I could not face Frau Brandjen and give her the smashed cake. I could not bear to disappoint her. I could not bear to see her disappointment and lose her good will. I could not bear the pain. The man eventually rode off, while I sat on the ground a while longer in utter hopelessness.

Finally I picked myself up and arrived home in despair and shame. I was resigned to the fact that I had failed and was unlovable. My mother was softened by my obvious misery, which was so deep that I could not hide it from her. She asked me if I wanted her to give the cake to Frau Brandjen, and I accepted and was grateful that I did not have to face her. For future holidays, Frau Brandjen still ordered the delicate mocha layer cake from the baker, but she never again asked me to pick it up for her. She came to our house occasionally and I heard her talk, but she never again addressed me with those sweet words that were like candy to my heart.

From the time I was about six and maybe earlier, I was expected to help out when the cattle were driven from the meadow where they had finished grazing to one with more succulent grass. My job would be to run ahead and position myself in the center of a driveway or in an open entry to a meadow and prevent the cows from straying off the path. Each time I was terrified. My knees would shake. My whole body would be in an uproar. But I told no one, as I knew only too well that the response would be, "You're afraid? You must be crazy to be afraid!"

When you are six years old, a mature cow is an awfully big animal. I was not afraid that a cow would hurt me. My father would break a switch off a tree and give it to me so that I could threaten or even hit any straying cow on the nose. All our cows were gentle unless they became fearful, frantic, and were driven out of control. I was afraid of that, that I might fail to control them and one would rush by me into a forbidden driveway or meadow. I would then be scolded or ridiculed, and I would feel as if I had failed, and that hurt. As long as I remained a child, cattle drives filled me with a fear that I bottled up inside and for which I had no outlet. Only when I became a teen-ager could I take a cattle drive in stride.

I felt equally frightened when I began milking cows on my own at the age of about twelve or thirteen. The first couple of months, I would sit under a cow and stoically clamp my knees around the pail to keep them from shaking. When I finally stood up, my knees would shake so badly that I could not walk. Again, I was afraid of the cow having her own will and walking away from me, and me not being in control. This fear left quickly, however, and this experience taught me that fear can be overcome. Soon I came to love being on a meadow alone with half a dozen cows, milking one after another, leaning my forehead against their big, warm bodies, and feeling a special atunement with nature all around me.

In spring and autumn planting and harvesting seasons, I often had to put my books aside after school and head for the fields to join my family in work. My body often hurt from the difficult labor. I had sore knees, a sore back, blistered hands, but my parents were always there, hurting also. Sometimes work was fun, as when we harvested potatoes. Four or five of us would crawl side by side on our hands and knees and collect potatoes into baskets. My father would pick up the full baskets and pour them onto the wagon. While we worked, we often played word games, such as ten questions, which my mother loved. She also made sure we always had plenty to eat during the breaks, which we took on a patch of heather under a cluster of birch trees. On the final day of the potato harvest, the break became a virtual party with store-bought coffee cake that had raisins, almonds, and thick sugar icing.

The most enchanting place to work was the large peat

bog in Grossenhain, where my father rented an acre or so of ground. Very few farmers still dug peat to use as fuel, and we were surrounded by many empty and silent plots. Heather, birch bushes, and trees grew along the ditches that separated the plots. Sounds of traffic from the paved road were muffled and far away. The quietness had a sacred feeling to it.

My father worked inside the six-foot-deep trench. He cut the peat into bricks and set them up in a row. Sometimes alone, but usually with a sister or brother, I loaded the wet peat bricks onto a wheelbarrow and carted them to the end of the plot. Here I set them out to dry and went back for another load. The aroma of fresh peat is unique, smelling of ancient forests, of ancient life that has decayed and transformed into a new and valuable substance. The texture of peat differs from smooth and oily in the layers on the bottom to coarse and grainy in the middle and dry and woody in the top layers.

In the afternoon we sometimes heard church bells ring but could not tell from what village the sound came. In the peat bog I saw snakes slither away and was not frightened. I watched birds feeding their young in nests in low bushes and was fascinated by a cloud of golden pollen adrift over a large field of rye on the edge of the peat bog. In the middle of our plot, partially hidden by birch bushes, was a square pit with dark water over which dragonflies chased each other in the midday sun. I loved to sit here after lunch while my father took a nap under a tree, his cap pulled over his eyes.

With the right training, I think my father would have made a fine artist. The pieces of peat he cut were identical in size and shape. When he plowed, his furrows were always straight. His haystacks never collapsed. He had a gentle temperament, delighting in his children and in healthy fields of corn and potatoes. When he spotted deer across the brook while haying with the family or a lark singing in the sky, he would stop raking the hay or plowing the field and call his children who were working alongside him and point out the animals to them.

I remember one afternoon when he, my sister Hanni, and I were digging peat for fuel and setting it up in long rows to dry. My father stood at the bottom of a pit that was 6' deep. Before him was an 18' wide wall of black, moist peat. Two male employees of my Uncle Jan, my mother's brother, walked over.

"Jan sent us over to look at your pit and your wall. He says ours is too uneven and we should learn from you how to do it right."

"Well, take a look then," said my father.

They looked and talked among themselves about how even the wall was and how identical in size and shape were the pieces of wet peat, like machine-cut bricks, that Papa set out on the edge for Hanni and me to cart away.

"How do you get the pieces so even?" one of them asked.

"How do you measure?" added the other.

"Measure?" my father echoed and smiled. "I don't measure. I just do it."

They could hardly believe it. But my father had an artist's eye for straight, natural, and efficient lines. It flowed out of him without effort. My uncle's employees went away shaking their heads. I learned that afternoon that my father had a particular skill in how his hands and eyes worked together. He could do something with ease and without effort that others could not do.

My father liked to play cards occasionally in the winter, and he loved to smoke cigarettes. My mother despised both, especially the cigarettes which she called "coffin nails," and she often complained that smoking would kill him. If this annoyed my father, he rarely let on. He had no other vices that I can think of and refused to give up his cigarettes.

Sometimes when my mother complained, picking on him or on one of the children, and spewed forth negativities in a rage born of frustration and despair, he treated her like a wise philosopher treats a misbehaving child.

"Do you hear what you are saying? Listen to yourself."

But my mother did not listen to herself, nor did she listen to my father. Because of her conditioning in childhood that men are the superior sex, they had a relatively peaceful relationship with each other. Any harsh words that were spoken were my mother's, often aimed at her children—me, in particular—and usually when my father was not around.

I was fortunate in that I grew up not only with one father figure in the house, but two—Heinrich, my paternal grandfather, whom I called Opa. Born in 1880, he was a child when his father died, and because the property was poorly managed by those the government had put in charge, he inherited nothing. He could not even go to school, but was a child laborer who helped his mother and siblings survive. Yet he was diligent, and before he and my grandmother married, he bought back his father's property. It was Grandmother who taught him to read and write. Through my childhood I was exposed to two types of masculine energy—my father's, which was gentle and peaceful, and my grandfather's powerful, selfish, and aggressive energy.

Opa was in his seventies when I became aware of him, and I liked him. That I shared a bed with my sister in my grandparents' bedroom and often heard his quiet, peaceful breathing may have contributed to feeling comfortable with him. I learned from my father's sister, Anna, that Grandfather had been a tyrant to his family in his younger days. She said he often picked on my father and beat him. By the time I knew him that kind of fight had gone out of him.

I remember Grandfather once swinging himself onto the saddle of a bike to ride to the dentist, and I was amazed that he could still do that. I also remember him coming home from long walks through the fields and meadows that he loved very much. Most of all, I remember a particular encounter with him when I was seven or eight years old. It was in the summer. I had bare legs and a boil on my left knee. Grandfather sat on the wooden bench in front of the house.

"Come here, let me take a look at that knee," he said.

I stood before him. He lifted my knee, grasped it between both of his knees, and inspected the fiery-looking boil.

"That needs to be lanced," he said and reached for his pocketknife. "No, don't worry. It won't hurt a bit," he added when he saw the terror in my eyes. Strangely, I trusted him. He wiped the knife on his corduroys and neatly sliced into the boil. He had been right; it didn't hurt at all. The pus ran out, and he sent me to Grandmother to clean it up.

"Go tell her to put something on it," he said.

The only time Opa spent days in bed was when he broke his leg on one of his long walks through the fields. It healed well and he lived to be eighty-three.

As a farmer, my father was around very much during my growing up years, and I did not mind that he expected me to help out with the work as soon as I was able. My father was easy to work with because he neither criticized nor complained, and he expected no more from anyone than that person could handle. What my father did not like, however, was for anyone to show pain. He ignored it or ridiculed and belittled the child who showed it. The first day of raking hay on the meadows with adult-sized wooden rakes invariably resulted in blisters for me and my brothers and sisters. My father's hands were tough and kept their calluses throughout the winter, but mine were young and soft. Often I had burning, open blisters on both hands after the first day of haying. Complaining was useless.

"So what?!" my mother and father would both say if I mentioned it. Neither one helped in putting on a soothing salve. Eventually the blisters healed and by the end of harvest I had four tough calluses on each hand. Both parents had the same response to back pain from spending a whole day or three days in a row bent over and putting potatoes into the ground. If I complained in the evening, "My back hurts," the response from both parents was invariably denial. "You're not even old enough to have a back."

Harvesting beets and turnips in late October and November in freezing temperatures while wearing rubber boots often led to frostbitten toes. Yet no doctor was ever called. "That will heal by itself," they said. One winter both of my big toes had holes on top from frostbite. I could even fit my fingertip into them. Eventually they healed, but for years the old wounds itched terribly every winter, including the first winter I was in New York.

One time riding home on my bike from work, with my father 100 yards behind me, my bike slipped on the narrow path. I crashed down onto the gravel and scraped my knees and the side of one leg. My knees and my leg burned with pain. Though I wanted to scream, I did not let my father know that I was suffering, afraid I would be ridiculed when I needed a kind word of comfort. Quick as the wind, I jumped back on the bike and pedaled off as if nothing had happened.

Another time I was cleaning an edible root with a sharp knife and accidentally cut into my thumb till the knife hit the bone. Today I would rush to the hospital and have it stitched up. Then, without a word to anyone, I quietly bandaged the wound. No one even asked about the bandage on my thumb. Fortunately it healed well, and only a thin white scar remains. My parents were true to the fundamentalist Lutheran tradition and believed that bodies were not to be pampered, but treated harshly as if somehow they had to pay for original sin.

From the age of thirteen, I occasionally experienced a

rapid heartbeat that made breathing difficult and my knees weak. Believing that it was my own fault or that God was punishing me for something, I delayed telling my parents. They must have thought that since I could still walk, was not screaming from pain, and was not bleeding, there was no reason for concern. The next time the doctor was in the house for someone who was "really" ill, I urged my mother to ask him about my rapid heartbeat. She did and, without examining or even asking me, he prescribed a tonic which had no effect. Subsequently I frequently continued my work on the farm with the rapid heartbeat and told no one.

My mother's behavior squelched my ability to express my good feelings, and my father's behavior squelched my ability to express my painful feelings. If I had not received the love of my grandmother, friendships with Birgit, Christa, and Rosemarie, I might have grown up living from my mind but emotionally dead. I must have recognized the love that I received as the real value because I isolated the pain, undigested, unassimilated, inside my body and mind. When I was an adult, economically independent and self-sufficient, my difficulties with relationships became so painful that I was desperate. I looked for help from dreaded authority figures—professional therapists—and found support and relief. I also found my way to esoteric schools and organizations and discovered a new way of looking at life and experiences that empowered me. Studying the ancient esoteric wisdom, I recognized my true identity as a human female being and consciously set a purpose and goal for my life.

In 1959, when I was sixteen, a young girl named Monika moved to our village when her widowed mother took a job here as housekeeper for a widower and his children. Monika spoke *Plattdeutsch* as well as anyone in the village, and we quickly became friends. One Sunday afternoon we took one of our many long walks on a quiet road outside the village. I asked her about something I had been thinking about, something I imagined every young girl contemplated.

"Why do you think you're here?" I said and added, "What do you think life is all about?"

If it had not been for her answer, which shocked me, I would not remember this conversation. She said, "I never think about that. Maybe I'll think about that when I'm thirty-five, but maybe I'll never think about it."

How could that be? How could anybody live and not question the meaning of existence? I often did.

Who was I? Just another person, exchangeable? The accidental result of a sperm and an egg coming together? My mother's little slave? A girl without importance? I reflected on my last year in grammar school. Herr Bokelmann, our teacher, prided himself on knowing the future of his students. He said Christa would be married by the time she was eighteen and Rosemarie by the time she was twenty (he was right about both), but he could not see what Jennifer would do. Neither could I see what I would do or what particular desires for my future I had. Life seemed to be something that just happened to me.

Once when we were in the small bedroom that Monika shared with her mother, she complained to me about her mother's demands and expectations, and I secretly envied her for the very same things she complained about. Her mother saw her and paid positive attention to her. I wished that my mother would make those demands on me and have those expectations. The picture I saw was of a mother who cared very much about her daughter and wanted the best for her. I saw a mother-daughter relationship that was alive, vibrant, full of communication and feelings, including love and caring.

I thought of my own relationship with my mother and I cried bitterly, not out of envy, but out of grief. I mourned our relationship that had none of those characteristics, but instead was cold, hostile, uncaring, and hurtful. It was a bitter relationship, and bitter tears flowed. Monika had consoled me as best as she could.

Later, sitting in Monika's living room in Germany in 1987, we listened to carefree songs of adventure and romance on the North Sea, which were popular when we were teenagers. We had danced with our boy friends many times to these songs from a jukebox in a little cafe in Bremerhaven. The songs and melodies had added sweetness to those years. Some of them I had not heard since I left Germany in 1961. Perhaps Monika was thinking of my old pain when she presented me with those two albums to take back to the States. Naturally, I treasure them.

During the years I grew up, my mother was dutifully neighborly with our farming neighbors, but she never had a really close friend, the way I define a close friend. My father was more social and had male friends whom he liked playing cards with and others with whom he sang in the choir. My mother often criticized his friends for smoking too much, but eventually she developed a friendship with the wife of one of his friends.

My mother's relationship with her mother-in-law was not close and was beset with many small resentments and disappointments. Oma was genteel and came from a family of teachers and ministers. Grandmother also had easy and natural social graces and was a popular woman who easily attracted people and enjoyed conversations with them. My mother, on the other hand, was competitive in everything she did.

My sisters were three, five, and seven years older than I, yet I had practically no emotional relationship with them as a child. We worked together more than we played together. In school they pretended not to know me. I remember feeling envious of them because, due to their ages, they had privileges that I did not have. I used to blame my mother for my sisters' indifference to me. Since she thought so little of me, I figured that they were imitating her. Thinking back on it, I think my sensitivity and dependency colored the picture. Had I been an aggressive and selfish child, I would have experienced them differently. One sister, however, Hanni, made an impression on me when I was a child.

She had not winced when a mysterious Santa Claus put her in his sack one Christmas and carried her out of the house. Later, Hanni said: "I knew who it was. It was our neighbor, Herr Ratje." Also, she could jump over the bottom part of the farm door in one leap and received a lot of attention for this feat from our mother. By the time I was eleven, she had finished grammar school and hired herself out for the summer to work on a nearby estate. Week after week she would tell me all about working, harvesting turnips as big as basketballs. Instead of knives, we used old World War I period swords to harvest root vegetables on our farm.

"They lie in a long line on the ground and you take your sword, lift it up, and slice cleanly between the fat root and the green tops. Again and again and again. Well, last night I dreamed that I was doing that, but instead of turnips in one line lay all the people I didn't like." She laughed.

"And I took that sword, lifted it up high—and cut off all of their heads." She laughed again.

My sister's energy was similar to my mother's, but with Hanni I felt safe. Her aggression was playful. In her relationships with people she was not motivated to attack and injure, but to create a safe distance. What this dream meant to her, I don't know. Perhaps it meant that it was O.K. to have power and to be aggressive. I did not have that power, I was terrified of it, but I wished I could be that fearless. Hanni's dream showed me a way of thinking that I could not conceive of in my frightened, vulnerable mind. Her dream was a gift to me in that it showed me the other end of the extreme—she was too aggressive where I was too timid. I think it is easier to make an adjustment toward the middle when you know what both extremes are.

I believe that my present associations with my sisters are creating connections of a deeper nature. All five of us share the experience of living in an adopted country and having memories of another. We stick together now, also with our brothers—not particularly warm and loving, but familiar and trusting companions. I would not be surprised to meet any one of my sisters in a future life and have an instant good relationship with her.

By the age of sixteen I was a pretty but shy farm girl. In the village I was known was "Johann Borchers' daughter, the fourth one." I had no sense of my own identity and believed I was in the world to please other people. I felt entitled to nothing except that which accidentally came my way. I was withdrawn, but craved knowledge and read every book and every newspaper I could get my hands on.

In my relationships with my friends I was passive and accommodating. I could not verbalize my feelings, nor could I express my wishes. I was smart, I could listen, but I talked little. Neighbors and relatives said about me, "Still waters run deep." I felt like a stranger in the physical world, but it was the only world I knew about. I did not act out the pain and anger I had hidden deep inside of me, but kept a tight lid on them and perfectly repressed all my feelings.

Chapter 2
Crossings

Though nothing can bring back the hour
Of splendor in the grass, of glory in the flower;
We will grieve not, rather find
Strength in what remains behind.
—(From: *Intimations of Immortality*, by William Wordsworth)

DURING seventh and eighth grade, I remember discussing s-e-x with my classmates, Christa and Rosemarie, and we even drew pictures of what we thought a couple making love would look like. We couldn't figure out, though, where the baby would come out and opted finally for the mother's belly button. We thought it would magically unfold. Secretly, we read a two-page story that was being circulated in class, called "The Wedding Night," a colorful and dramatic description of intercourse. A few years earlier, our head teacher, beloved Herr Tscheuschner, a very proper, highly educated man with high morals and great dedication to teaching, had discovered "The Wedding Night" among a student's papers. He had been hurt, disappointed, and enraged that "his" students would read such filth. It had been a minor scandal in the village. Everybody who knew about the incident seemed to sympathize with Herr Tscheuschner. We were extremely careful when we circulated the story from that point on.

In my house sex was never mentioned. When I menstruated for the first time, I told my grandmother, not my mother. One day, at age thirteen or fourteen, I discovered a medical book underneath some clothes on the bottom of the clothes closet. The book contained a section on sexuality, including pictures of human sexual anatomy, and described what happened during the sex act. I sneaked into the closet many times and studied the information. At least I knew the facts. Later, it turned out that my mother had left the book there on purpose because she could not talk about sex. My older sisters had also independently discovered the book and sneaked in to study it.

On the farm, sex was all around me. Chickens, geese, and turkeys copulated freely in the farmyard. My father took the cows to the village bull or had them artificially inseminated by the veterinarian. When the veterinarian had been there once, I may have been around twelve, I casually picked up the insemination record and absent-mindedly read some of the words that appeared there. " . . . age . . . last time . . . eggs . . . " My father overheard me and said, laughing, "What? Cows lay eggs?" But I, of course, was mortified that he had caught me reading it.

I graduated from grammar school in April 1958 at age fourteen. By then, Heinz, Catharina, and Bertha had already emigrated to the U.S., and Hanni followed that spring. Ever since I was twelve, I, too, thought of following the family tradition that had begun with my grandmother and her two sisters who had emigrated to the U.S. in 1899. My father's brother and three sisters emigrated between 1922 and 1935. Because my grandfather had forbidden my father to leave

Germany and insisted that he take over the farm, my father vowed to let his children do whatever they wanted to do. If they wished to leave, he would not stop them, and my mother agreed with him.

From 1958 to 1961, with the exception of one winter, I worked on my parents' farm. I was then the oldest in the house. By then, I was inured to my mother's cruelties, although she had also mended her ways somewhat. There was hardly anything I didn't do on the farm. I worked in the house with my mother, cooking and cleaning, and in the fields and meadows with my father. I planted potatoes, collected the ugly bugs that were eating and damaging the plants, harvested potatoes, raked the weeds from between fields of beets and turnips, raked hay, and bound freshly mowed rye and barley into sheaves. With the exception of two strong oxen, the work on our farm was done by hand. In winters, the cows and oxen had to be fed and watered with buckets of water pumped from a pump in our kitchen.

My favorite work as a teen-ager was milking the cows. In winter they stood in a warm stall, but in summer they grazed on meadows near the Geeste, a stream that flowed a mile from our house. The cows were my emotional mother more than my mother ever was. They generously gave every drop of milk they produced, their big bodies exuded warmth, and they were always calm and patient. As I milked one cow after another, all alone on the meadow, often a deer would pop out of the woods. I could hear birds in the nearby trees and would sense the invisible life not only in the animals around me, but also in the grass, in the bushes, and in the trees. I sensed that there was another realm besides the physical, but at the time I had no words with which to describe it.

During the fall of 1959 my parents hired me out to Mother's brother and his wife, Uncle Jan and Aunt Tine, who owned one of the largest farms located at the other end of the village. The money I earned, however, was mine. My uncle had horses, and my cousin Dietrich and I sometimes went riding. My cousin Käthe was two years older than I and we got along pleasantly. For the first time in my life I not only had my own bed, but my own room, containing, however, only a bed, a closet, and a chair. Still, it was mine, and for the first time in my life I had privacy. Now I could not, however, sneak away with a newspaper or book I had borrowed, and read secretly when I was supposed to work, the way I had done at home. My aunt and uncle were good people and treated me well. An older neighbor of ours with a terrific sense of humor, named Uncle Stüve, worked for my uncle, and he never failed to make me laugh by making light of a heavy work load.

On Saturdays during those years, there was often a dance in Köhlen or in a village nearby. I and my friends, usually Christa and Rosemarie, would go there and dance with the young men. My mother had sent me to dancing school when I was fourteen, and I enjoyed dancing the waltz, polka, and tango.

On the Sunday afternoon before Christmas in 1959 I met Christa in the village square to go for a walk. With her was a young man, Franz-Heinz Quadhammer, whom Christa had been dating. He stood relaxed, wearing a leather jacket, and grinned pleasantly. His eyes were bright and, when they met mine, I immediately felt comfortable with him. Our walk that day was short. During a moment when Christa had stepped away, Franz asked me to go dancing with him the following Saturday. I felt compelled to say yes, even though he was Christa's boy friend and this might be the end of our friendship.

I told Christa during the week that Franz-Heinz had asked me for a date and that I had accepted. Was that all right with her? To my relief she said it was O.K. He was actually a distant cousin of hers, and her parents were not happy that she was dating him. At the time I had no idea what momentous role Franz-Heinz would play in my life for many years to come.

I dated Franz-Heinz all that winter and the following spring. In those days it was the custom in the villages for young people to date on Wednesdays and Saturdays. Franz-Heinz was the son of a farmer two villages away. He was twenty-one years old and would eventually inherit his father's farm. To gain more experience, he had coincidentally hired himself out to the farmer diagonally across the road from my uncle's farm where I was staying.

Every Wednesday night when the work was done and I had cleared away the dishes, Franz-Heinz came to pick me up. We usually walked arm in arm along the road to a nearby wood, called the Westernholz. There were no street lamps, but we easily found our way by moonlight or in the dark by flashlight. There was a place in the woods where in the summer a tent was put up by the Schützenverein (Shooting Club) for the biggest fair and dancing of the year. It was so quiet there in the woods at night, but the echoes of joyously dancing people seemed to hang in the air all around us. Sheltered by trees, we found a place to sit and talked for hours.

When I was with Franz, I felt like a different person. For the first time I felt that I was more than just somebody's "fourth daughter." Franz regarded me with unconditional positive regard, and his attention to me made me feel that I had value in my own right. I had never been much of a talker with my family and spoke little even with my friends, but with Franz there was never a moment of silence. With him, I did not feel empty inside with nothing to say. Talking with him was easy and natural. He never criticized me or what I said, and I never worried about saying the wrong thing. With him I felt like a normal and likable person. When he walked me home after our first date and kissed me good-by, I kept my body rigid and my lips tense. I was afraid to relax because I didn't know what feelings would come up.

"You don't know how to kiss," he said. "I will have to teach you." With infinite tenderness and sweetness he kissed me. His lips were warm and his arms gently encircled me. I relaxed and paid attention.

"How was that?" I asked.

"A little better," he said.

The following Saturday we went dancing in a nearby village. He picked me up on his BMW 800 motorcycle and the December air was cold. I wore slacks underneath my party dress and sweaters and a heavy coat over my dress. When I sat behind him on the motorcycle, he urged me to put my arms around his middle and hold on tight, but I was shy. In my family we did not touch each other unless absolutely necessary. However, I learned to cling to him tightly and to enjoy the closeness.

Franz did not have the best of reputations. His father was an alcoholic, and people said that Franz drank too much, too. They also said he was not faithful to his girlfriends. Franz liked to drink as much as he liked to dance and ride his motorcycle. He was a bit of a daredevil; however, I never saw him drunk. I always felt safe riding behind him on the bike, even when he drove me home from a dance at two or three in the morning. My aunt knew of his unsavory reputation and did everything she could to get us apart, but I defended him and loved him nonetheless.

One night he asked me about my relationship with my parents. I don't remember the specifics of what I told him, except that I had a painful relationship with my mother. It was easy to talk to him because with him I seemed to share a frame of reference I shared with no one else. I needed to say only very little, and he would guess, or intuit, the rest. I remember he told me that his parents preferred his younger sister. I could tell he felt neglected and hurt, but he consoled himself that he would one day inherit the farm.

One evening during the week I showed up unexpectedly at my parents' house after dark. As I entered the living room and greeted everyone, my mother, who knew the light on my bicycle was not working, asked, "How did you get here?"

I said, "Franz-Heinz brought me."

"And how will you get home?" she asked.

"He will pick me up at ten," I answered.

I expected my parents to warn me against Franz-Heinz or at least to tell me he was not good enough for me. I did not dare to hope, but dreamed anyway that one of them would insist on meeting him and checking him out for themselves—as loving parents did in novels. After all, I was only sixteen. Fat chance. Neither my mother nor father said anything about Franz. It seemed my parents cared less about me than my aunt did. I felt empty and ashamed.

A few months later Franz and I went to a dance in a neighboring village. We danced every dance with abandon. Franz was an excellent dancer and led with a gentleness so that I found it easy to follow his every step. We sailed easily through loopholes among other dancing couples and turned around and around ourselves in the same spot. We became hot and went outside for a breath of cool winter air. Standing in the shade of the building, we were shielded from the bright light that lit up the front yard. "I have thought about this," he said, "and I want to ask you something. Will you marry me?"

I was overjoyed, feeling like an inexperienced child and a wise old woman at the same time. I said, "Yes, I want to marry you. But I'm only sixteen. Let's wait until I'm twenty."

"That's fine," he said. "I'm twenty-one now. When you are twenty, I'll be twenty-five, and that is a good age for a man to settle down." We danced for the rest of the night and, after midnight, he took me home.

That night or on another night soon after, Franz playfully forced his way into my bedroom at my aunt's house. He lay in my bed and suggested that I join him. I stubbornly refused. I dare not think what would have happened had he tried to force me either physically or mentally. But he did not. He was indeed a *gentleman*. Eventually he got up and left and never tried it again.

I don't know why I kept our engagement a secret, but I did. I must have been afraid without being conscious of it. Perhaps I feared he would become an alcoholic like his father, perhaps I feared unfaithfulness and abandonment. Before long, I heard from girlfriends that they had seen him attend dances without me and spend time with girls who were "easy." I confronted him, and he promised it would not happen again. But it did. Before spring gave way to summer, he stopped calling on me on Wednesdays and Saturdays. We had no telephone, and the letter I sent him remained unanswered.

By summer I returned to my parents' farm, heartbroken. I brooded and moped. I could not share my pain with my parents. Only Christa knew I was upset by Franz's leaving, and she tried to get me news of what he was doing. Meanwhile, I worked on the farm and poured my pain into singing sad love songs and hymns from church. One hymn in particular, "In deep distress I cry to You, dear Lord, please hear my prayer," I sang over and over, but only when I was alone. Life continued. There was work to be done, and now I returned my attention to my earlier plan to emigrate to the States.

In 1960, Germany did not yet have the *Wirtschaftswunder*, or economic opportunities, for which it would later become famous. My brother and sisters did well in the States; they either owned a delicatessen or a restaurant or were partners in one. If I stayed in Germany, I had only one option: to work in a large farming household and later to marry a farmer. With the exception of Franz, I could not really see myself married to a farmer. I had not the foggiest idea of what awaited me in the States, but expected to follow in my sisters' footsteps—find employment as a housekeeper or delicatessen clerk, then marry someone and together build up a small business.

In October of 1960, my mother, father, and youngest brother Johann traveled to the U.S. They would stay until the end of March 1961. When Bertha was not with her husband, Karl, who was in the U.S. Army and stationed in Bavaria, she shared in the responsibility on the farm. Otherwise, Bernhard, Richard, Tina, and the house were under my care. I turned seventeen in November and matured that winter in spite of my grief over losing Franz.

I particularly remember being "midwife" to two of our pregnant cows, supervising their calving and delivering two strong, healthy calves. When the first calf's hoofs showed, I sent Bernhard to run to a neighbor for help—which is the same my father would have done. While he was gone, I made sure I knew where the schnapps bottle was and that a clean glass was on hand. Next, I prepared a rope and placed clean straw in front and in back of the calving cow. When our neighbor came, I led him to the rear of the stall. One of us placed the rope around the calf's slippery hooves and together we pulled each time the cow heaved. When the calf slipped out, we grasped it by its slimy hoofs and placed it in the clean straw before the happy cow. She licked it dry. All stood and admired the big, healthy calf.

Imitating my father, I brought out the schnapps bottle and gratefully offered a shot glass of schnapps to everyone who participated, except the children. I was extremely conscious of doing a "man's" job and very proud that my father trusted me to do it. Furthermore, I was very pleased that our neighbor, who had often irritated me with sexist remarks about this or that boyfriend, accepted the schnapps from me with grace and respect.

Around October of 1960, Franz-Heinz's formal engagement to another girl had been published in the local newspaper. I thought my heart would break. But New Year's Eve I met him at a dance which he attended without his fiancée, and he danced only with me. For a long time that night we sat side by side in the champagne bar, and I felt transported out of time and place into a dimension of eternal love and peace. We were the last couple to leave the ballroom at five in the morning, and he drove me home on his motorcycle. I felt that he loved me, and I still loved him, but I could not tell him so.

When we arrived at the farm, I invited him in for breakfast. I didn't have to milk the cows that morning because my sister Bertha, visiting from the States, was relieving me. I heard her milking a steady stream into the metal pail as I led Franz into the kitchen. We ate breakfast and felt each others' presence but talked little. Half an hour later I stood beside him in the front yard as he straddled his motorcycle and was about to turn on the motor. "I hear you are going to get married," I said.

"Yes," he said. "I hear you are going to America."

"Yes," I said. With neither a kiss nor a handshake, we parted.

The special responsibility I had that winter, the brief joy of seeing Franz again, and the unconscious anxiety of my impending departure made the winter a very vivid experience. Two days after my parents would return from New York in March, I would leave Germany on the same boat. When I performed certain chores, I asked myself how many more times would I do this. When I visited certain places in our fields and meadows that were dear to me, I asked if I would ever see them again. Even when I saw some person from the village whom I did not see very often, I asked if this were the last time I would see that person. Franz-Heinz was not the only one my heart had to say good-by to.

I left Germany by boat on the first day of April 1961.

Friends and relatives drove me to Bremerhaven in a VW bus. We stood on the wooden deck planks of the S.S. *Bremen*, and I remember vividly my mother and father awkwardly shaking my hand good-by. Not a hug, not a word of advice. I expected something from both of them and felt empty that nothing was given. I wondered if I were expecting too much, but I did not think so. I intuitively perceived that my mother and father, standing there before me on the wooden planks of the ship, were emotionally crippled. I did not understand at the time how much their handicaps had affected me and crippled me as well.

Crossing the Atlantic on the *Bremen*, I traveled blindly into the future. I was not particularly afraid. I knew there was a job waiting for me, and a brother and three sisters lived within twenty miles of where I would be staying. Perhaps my strongest feeling was one of relief that I would be far away from my mother and safe from her negative energies. I also had a secret hope that, because my mother would not be there, I would be closer to my sisters, and we would be able to care about each other like friends.

The days aboard the *Bremen* were a luxury which I had never experienced before. In the dining room the tables were covered with white linen tablecloths, and the food I chose from a fancy menu was served by waiters in tuxedos. Two theaters played films, and every evening there was dancing. The view from the upper deck where I saw nothing but ocean to the very horizon in every direction and the smell of salt in the air were unforgettable. After five days at sea, the *Bremen* came into New York harbor and passed beneath the unfinished Verrazano Bridge. Workmen on the bridge leaned against the railing, looked down, and waved to us, and the passengers on the boat waved back. That was my first experience in America. My brother Heinz, who had sponsored my immigration, picked me up by car from the boat. We drove underneath the Henry Hudson Parkway, and

I thought how ugly the city was.

For the first week I stayed with Heinz, his wife, Klara, and their two small children in a cramped apartment above their delicatessen in Rosedale, Queens. Whenever I left the apartment, I stepped onto a cement sidewalk and was assaulted by the sounds of an endless stream of hasty automobiles. I immediately missed the garden, orchard, and meadows of home. I was suffering culture shock, and my sensitive psyche shut down for some time from an overload of impressions.

After a week, I went to work as a housekeeper and governess in Catharina's household. Kati, as she now called herself, lived in a spacious second floor apartment in Massapequa, Long Island, and together with her husband, Otto, was a partner in a restaurant in town. I delighted in my own room with bed, chair, and dresser, and a window that led out onto a flat roof. While my sister went to work, I did the housekeeping and watched over my pretty little nieces, two-year-old Ellen and three-week-old Linda. My English consisted of one year of instruction in Oxford English at grammar school, and little Ellen spoke more words than I did. She was my first real American English teacher.

One morning during my fourth week, as Ellen played on the rug in the living room and Linda dozed in her crib, I heard the mailman drop envelopes through the slot in the door. I went downstairs and picked them up. One was an airmailed letter from my mother. Sitting on the lowest step, I opened it. A newspaper clipping fell out. It was an obituary announcing that Franz-Heinz was dead at the age of twenty-two years from a motorcycle accident. I went rigid with shock and sat for a while, uncomprehending.

I learned that he had married a month before my ship sailed for the States. His wife had been pregnant with his child when they married and had just given birth to a baby girl in May. After visiting her in the hospital for the third time, he rode home on his motorcycle, lost control, and smashed into a tree. He was found dead the next morning.

I shared the news with my sister that evening and expected her to comfort and reassure me. But she thought I was being sentimental. I did not feel emotionally safe to tell her what Franz-Heinz meant to me and how much I had loved him. I told her only that he had been my friend. I sensed, but could not put it into words, that my relationship with him was meaningful beyond my comprehension. My initial hope that without my mother around my relationships with my sisters would be warm and supportive of my feelings was dashed.

I was still a Lutheran and supposed to believe that someone who dies goes either to heaven or to hell. On the outside, Franz-Heinz had not lived a good life. Like his father, he drank too much. He went to every dance in the county he heard about, drove his motorcycle too fast, and was unfaithful to his girlfriends. But I still loved him, felt loved by him, and I could not condemn him. The shock of his death gave me pause to think. Was he supposed to go to hell because he drank too much, wasn't faithful to women, and rode a fast motorcycle? What about the influence on him of his father's alcoholism and both parents' rejection of him in favor of his sister? I could not believe that God, if He existed, would send him to hell. The hymn, "In deep distress I cry to You, dear Lord, please hear my prayer," that had so comforted me six months earlier, now left a bitter taste in my mouth. I was disappointed with Lutheranism, with the theory of God, and I became an atheist for several years. I did not know at the time that God was patient and would wait for me to return.

I enjoyed taking care of Ellen and Linda, and I sang to them frequently. But I found housework a tedious bore, and I felt isolated out on Long Island. After eighteen months I switched places with Lene, who was working in Heinz's delicatessen in Rosedale, Queens. I moved into a boarding house in Jamaica, sharing a large sunny room with another German girl. This house belonged to a widow who was Yugoslavian by birth. She rented eight or nine rooms and attracted people from all over the world. We called it the "international house." Tenants came from China, Japan, Indonesia, Iceland, Germany, France, and the U.S., and we shared a communal kitchen. I was shy, but I enjoyed the international flavor. I wanted to learn better English in order to pass the test for citizenship and signed up for classes that were being given in the vocational high school on Hillside Avenue in Jamaica, Queens.

Long Island had an active German community in the early sixties. The Plattdeutsche Park Restaurant in Franklin Square was headquarters for numerous German clubs. My family belonged to the Bederkesa Club and the Women's Choir. I joined the Bederkesa Club and the Dance Club. There were open dances galore on Saturdays. I also frequently got together with my family on Christmas, Thanksgiving, and other holidays. My sisters and brothers were having babies, and eventually I would have eighteen nieces and nephews. My sisters and oldest brother married when they were twenty years old, and I was often told that I was expected to follow in that pattern. But I would shake my head, "I don't have to do what you did."

At first I dated a young man named Karl, then Dieter, both very good people, but when they came too close to me and seemed to have thoughts of marriage, I withdrew. I also dated Jerry a few times, the American-born son of a German couple who were partners in my sister's restaurant. Jerry attended college in Ohio, mostly paid for by his parents. I envied him the pleasure of four full years of doing nothing but learn at a university in Dayton. I felt sorry for myself for having to earn my own living, and out of the envy and self-pity a dream was born: to attend an American college. That way I could prove to myself that I was an intelligent and normal human being.

After working for my brother for eighteen months, I felt discontented and restless. My brother was a comfortable employer, but I did not like cooking meat pies over a hot stove and being splattered with cooking grease. I felt too smart to be a delicatessen clerk and wanted to work in an office. So I quit, left the boarding house, and first spent three leisurely months in Germany visiting my parents, relatives, friends, and my favorite places in the meadows and fields.

While there, I was also visited by Mr. John Spotts, whom I had befriended on the voyage from New York to Bremerhaven. He and his friend had been on their way to visit Germany, Switzerland, and Austria, and we had adjacent deck chairs on board. He was pleasant looking, very relaxed, and had an easy manner about him that made me trust him. He also had a sense of humor and liked to make me laugh. Besides, at first I thought he was a professor from Pennsylvania State College and I was very impressed. He was actually a talented carpenter and lived in State College next door to a church where he played the organ every Sunday. He was a widower, in his late sixties, and still missed his wife who had died a few years before.

He was fascinated with me for having grown up on a farm and was delighted when I invited him and his friend to visit us. They did, had coffee with my family, and he chatted (I thought he flirted) with my grandmother in English. He walked with me and my brothers to the peat bog to view peat pieces set out to dry in the sun. We took some photographs there. He told us that since his wife had died, his dream was to go to Africa and visit missionaries he knew from his church and help them with his carpentry. Before he left, he invited me to visit him and his other friends in State College.

When I returned to New York, I lived in Massapequa with

Kati for several months. She and her husband had recently bought a house on a quiet street in Massapequa with a front lawn, porch, and back yard. Now I filled in, again as housekeeper, for Lene who had gone on an extended trip to Germany. Linda was no longer dependent on the stroller, and she, Ellen, and I could walk together longer distances. When Lene returned, I needed a job. What was I going to do? I did not want to be a housekeeper, nor a waitress, nor a delicatessen clerk. I traveled by train into Manhattan to employment agencies looking for a job in an office. I wanted to work from nine to five, have my weekends free, and keep my hands clean while I worked. My family advised me against working in Manhattan because they thought the city was too dangerous a place for a young girl like me, especially an immigrant. But I was irresistibly drawn to the city even though I was rejected again and again because I had no high school diploma and no office experience.

My sister never asked for money for room and board. "Stay as long as you like," she said. "I've got the room and I've got the food. No problem." But I felt bad for being a freeloader. Once again I jumped blindly into the future, rented a room in a two-family house in Jamaica so that it would be easier to travel to Manhattan. But I still had no high school diploma nor office experience. My money soon ran out, and for a week I lived on ketchup sandwiches. I was desperate. I needed a job, any job.

Finally, I answered an ad for a job in a factory. I appeared for the interview wearing a powder blue woolen spring coat with three-quarter-length sleeves I had bought especially for my trip to Germany. It was elegant in the extreme. The man who interviewed me looked at my coat and said: "Do you really want this job?" "Yes" I said and started the next day. For the next two weeks, from nine to five, I sat on a stool at a table among other women, most of whom spoke no English, and stuffed black plastic spiders into one-inch plastic bubbles. I think they were put into slot machines as booby prizes.

The building in which I lived was owned by a family who occupied the first floor. I shared the second floor with a woman from France and a man from Iraq: Madeleine and Razkallah. Neither of our rooms had refrigerators or stoves, and cooking was actually forbidden except on one little hot plate. Razkallah did not enjoy cooking; Madeleine and I did. Madeleine and I had no money; Razkallah, who was an engineer, did. So, we fell into the habit that Razkallah bought food for a nice Saturday or Sunday meal. Madeleine and I gathered in his room with our hot plates, cooked a meal, and the three of us enjoyed it together.

I shared my woe with Razkallah about my spider job and ketchup sandwiches. "What am I going to do?" I asked.

"Very simple," said Razkallah. "You tell them you have a high school diploma."

"But if they want to see it?" I asked.

"Tell them it is lost," he said. "You will look for it. You will bring it later."

"All right," I said, "maybe they will buy it. But I have no experience."

"Ah, not important," said my engineering friend. "Make it up. Tell them you worked in an office in Germany. They will never check. And if they do, by then they will depend on your work, because you will do such a good job. I know you, you will, and they will be happy to have you."

I had been brought up to be scrupulously honest, but I was desperate, and ultimately I listened to Razkallah. I applied for the job as file clerk at Manufacturers Hanover Trust Company, a major bank on Park Avenue. A very nice woman in personnel gave me a test and then said: "You did very well, too good for a file clerk. I will hire you as a remittance clerk. It pays five dollars more per week."

My lies were found out, however. Not about high school,

but about my invented experience. The woman from personnel, I've forgotten her name but still see her face clearly in my mind, wrote to the company in Bremerhaven that I said I had worked for. She received a reply that they had never heard of me. She called me to her office, twice, and confronted me. I insisted I worked there and claimed they must have lost my papers. I believe she even confronted me a third time. Because I was so scared, I put on a good act, and she wanted to believe me. Eventually she shook her head and sent me back to my work station. I don't recommend fibbing to anyone, even if you feel you are qualified and believe, as I did, that a piece of paper is only a piece of paper. The insecurity and the fear of being found out are very unpleasant.

After eight months at the bank, my colleague, red-headed Mary, had become my friend. She had excellent secretarial skills acquired in high school and took a job as stenographer at the *New York Daily News.* She called me the following week and told me there was another job opening and why didn't I apply for it so we could still work together. I asked her what kind of job it was, and she said one just like hers. With typing and stenography and answering the telephone? Yes. By then I had taught myself to type and took a speed typing course at the YWCA, but I knew no stenography and speaking English on the telephone with fast talking Americans simply terrified me. I told her it made no sense for me to apply because I didn't have the skills. She said, "O.K. Then just come down for the interview. It'll be a good experience for you."

I thought it was silly, but I wanted to please her, and so I did. I passed the interview in the personnel department and was sent to the advertising department to meet Mary's supervisor. We had a nice little chat, but my heart dropped to the floor when she said, "Here is a pad and pencil. I want to dictate a little letter."

If I had told her the truth, I would have felt ashamed to embarrass my friend. So, I wrote down every word she said in longhand. It was easy. When she finished dictating, she asked to see my outlines.

"What is this?" she said. "You wrote it in longhand. Why?"

"Oh, I'm just too nervous during a test," I ventured. "But I got everything you said."

"O.K., type it up. I want to see how you set up a letter."

That was no problem either. I was by this time an excellent speller, and I had an eye for arranging words on a page so the effect was pleasing. She looked at the finished letter and said: "Good. You can start in two weeks."

I was in a daze. I walked out of the building and into the nearest bookstore and bought a book on Pitman stenography. For the next two weeks, I practiced Pitman shorthand every free minute. Two weeks later, I began working for four salesmen, all of whom were pleasant to work with. I experienced massive anxiety taking down shorthand notes and spelling names from telephone messages. After six months, Mary told me that our supervisor had confided in her: "The first three months I wasn't sure if Jennifer was going to make it. But now she is one of my best stenographers."

I obtained two promotions within four years and stayed at the newspaper for eleven years. It was about a month after starting to work there that I discovered a book by Gina Cerminara that seemed to reawaken mysterious memories in me of some ancient philosophy. I had gone for a long slow walk in Queens, in spite of a heat wave, and unexpectedly came across a little public library. I wandered among stacks of books, with hardly anybody else around except the librarian, and enjoyed the air-conditioned rooms. I was twenty-one years old by then, and four years had passed since I arrived in New York.

I browsed through the book with deep excitement, charged it out, and took it home. With my eighth-grade education and still inadequate English, I struggled to understand what Gina Cerminara wrote in *Many Mansions*, but I picked up two main concepts immediately—reincarnation and karma. Dr. Cerminara wrote about an American named Edgar Cayce who had a curious gift: He would put himself into a self-induced hypnotic trance and then know things about people, why they were sick and how they could be healed. He died in 1945, but left behind a body of over 14,000 multipage readings covering every imaginable subject. (A reading is the text of what he said to his questioners while he was in the trance. Each reading is identified by a number.) Sometimes he would reveal that their sickness had been caused by their own behavior—in a past lifetime. If we all had past lives, I wondered, would we also have future lives? Then nobody would go to heaven or hell for all eternity as Lutheranism taught.

So, if reincarnation were true, Franz-Heinz wasn't going to hell after all. He wasn't going to heaven either, but that was all right and very just. He would have another chance to learn to right the mistakes he had made this time around. The fact that he died at the young age of twenty-two didn't mean it was an accident—quite the contrary; his soul may well have chosen to die because he had either accomplished what he set out to do or circumstances had changed and he couldn't achieve his goals in this life. I found comfort in thinking that in some future life I would see him again and that we might have the opportunity to finish what we had begun. Maybe we would be able to get married and raise a family.

Reading *Many Mansions* led me to other metaphysical books and to membership in the Association for Research and Enlightenment, Inc. (A.R.E.), the organization founded by Edgar Cayce in 1931 in Virginia Beach, Virginia. Through the A.R.E., I suddenly had access to many different kinds of metaphysical information, meditation, biblical insights, right attitudes, dream interpretation, and psychic phenomena. None of this information was foreign to me. Quite the contrary, I felt that I had known it all before and was rediscovering it. I soon became absorbed in a book entitled *There Is a River,* the first biography of Edgar Cayce, by Thomas Sugrue. I would read with passion until late at night and on weekends, sometimes until the sun rose. Then I would climb through the window onto a slanted roof and watch the sun rise over the town below.

The metaphysical philosophy section in *There Is a River* fascinated me. In this new light, my Lutheran fundamentalist beliefs no longer held up. According to Edgar Cayce, God did not use sickness, sadness, and pain to punish us in an attempt to change our natural state of stupidity and sinfulness into one of enlightenment and goodness. Cayce said that God created our souls to be His companions. He created us like Himself: spirit, mind, individuality; cause, action, and effect. I learned that reincarnation is part of God's plan in which a soul exercises its own will and creates like God Himself. The cycle of reincarnation is completed when the soul has exhausted its separateness and realizes that God's will is the only will and voluntarily rejoins God in His divine consciousness. At that time I was especially struck by the following passage from *There Is a River:*

"Each soul enters the material plane not by chance, but through the grace, the mercy, of a loving Father; that the soul may, through its own choice, work out those faults, those fancies, which prevent its communion and at-onement with the Creative Forces.

"As to whether a soul is developed or retarded during a particular life depends on what the person holds as its ideal, and what it does in its mental and material relationships about that ideal.

"Life is a purposeful experience, and the place in which a

person finds himself is one in which he may use his present abilities, faults, failures, virtues, in fulfilling the purpose for which the soul decided to manifest in the three-dimensional plane." (Revised edition, seventeenth printing, April 1967, p. 380.)

I would often stop reading and reflect. The statement that "Life is a purposeful experience" stopped me in my tracks because this was new to me. My life, then, was not a meaningless accident as I had been thinking? I was not here to sacrifice myself for others, degrading myself, asking nothing for myself? If life was a purposeful experience, what was the purpose? I learned that I was not here to hate myself, but to love myself. Self-condemnation, said Edgar Cayce, was one of the worst sins we could commit. Our real purpose here on the Earth, he said, was to become better human beings, symbolically to follow in the footsteps of Christ, by loving the people in our daily lives more and more.

I was reading for the first time about the value of the human soul and the human being. Apparently Edgar Cayce never once admonished anyone, as I had so often been told, "You are so bad, you should feel ashamed of yourself." Quite the contrary. In one of Cayce's psychic readings (1825-1), he told the one who had come for advice, "For each soul is as precious in the sight, the heart of the Creator as if it were thine own blood in thine own material body."

Nowhere in the readings did Cayce indicate that women were worth less than men. Since a soul could inhabit a male body in one life and a female body in another, it was evident that men and women have the *same* value. The soul itself was androgynous, he said—neither male nor female.

Intuitively I understood this philosophy as correct and from deep within my mind, heart, and soul came a positive, excited response of joy and recognition. Growing up in an oppressive environment, the effects of which I would not understand for many years to come, made fully integrating this new philosophy into my everyday consciousness a slow process. Some parts of my mind resisted this new knowledge. I already felt different from other people because I was an immigrant, too sensitive, deep, and did not talk much. Being different hurt. I would have liked to be "the girl next door," have a smooth personality, fit in everywhere, and effortlessly get along with other people.

If I talked to my brothers and sisters about reincarnation, they were likely to say, "Yeah, and the moon is made of cheese." Mary sometimes humored me and let me talk about what I was reading, but her Catholic upbringing in Brooklyn permeated her beliefs. There was no room in her mind for reincarnation, karma, past or future lives.

After eight months at the *Daily News*, Mary left for a better paying job at a law firm, but I stayed on. I liked dealing with words and pictures at the newspaper, I found my colleagues kind and accepting of me, and I liked pursuing my hobby of reading during hours of privacy on my free evenings and weekends. With another friend, Haydee, from Argentina, whom I had met in an English class, I traveled to Washington, D.C., on a three-day weekend to get to know the nation's capital. I was twenty-two. After rejecting Dieter and Karl, I was beginning to have second thoughts about marriage.

Chapter 3
Illusions

Lead me from darkness into Light.
From the unreal to the Real.
From death to Immortality.
—(Rig Veda)

ON my return trip to New York from my visit home in 1964 aboard the *Bremen*, I had met a handsome young officer, Joachim. He was the bursar and made a dashing picture in his navy uniform with the gold buttons. I was as much in love with his uniform as with him. It was important to me at the time that he was socially correct in every way, which Franz had not been. Joachim knew how to make a good impression. He worked with people every day and related easily and smoothly with everyone. He seemed not ever to have suffered, and pain or problems never entered his conversations. This attitude on his part helped me forget my painful childhood and the difficulties I dealt with as an intelligent, but uneducated immigrant. Joachim was my "prince charming" who would lead me into a painless life of social correctness.

We met whenever the boat anchored in New York, which was every three weeks. Soon Joachim asked me to marry him and I said yes. He requested that I live with him in Bremerhaven after we were married, and I agreed. Still, I wondered if the pattern begun with my very first love, Detlef, at the age of six was going to repeat itself once again. Detlef had suddenly moved away with his family. My second love, Franz-Heinz, abandoned me, too. Would Joachim follow the same pattern?

When Joachim would arrive in New York, I would go to the pier to meet him. Either he would come with me to Queens, where I now rented my own little apartment, or I would spent the night with him on board. One early Sunday morning after I had shared his bed for the first time, I walked across Manhattan, which was nearly bereft of traffic. I was feeling that now I was a woman. There followed a glorious time in our relationship when I felt initiated into womanhood.

Joachim was very romantic, loved bringing me little gifts, and enjoyed dinner with me by candlelight. Months later, he asked me about my experience with him during sex. I enjoyed being intimate with him more than I had enjoyed anything else previously, but he did not ask that. He specifically asked if I experienced an orgasm. We had never discussed sex before, and I replied that I had not. He was more experienced than I, and I was not his first partner. I expected him to explain something to me or discuss it further, but, although he seemed upset, he said nothing. Amazingly, I never heard from him again after that.

I was surprised that it was so important to him. I felt that he either blamed me or that he blamed himself. Even in those days I knew that a repressive upbringing leaves tension in the body that delays sexual pleasure. I knew intuitively that there was nothing wrong with me; it was merely a matter of time. (I was right about that; a few years later Joachim would have received a different answer.) It was he who was both ignorant and unloving. Perhaps it was a blessing that he left. To pretend that I had experienced an orgasm when I did not never occurred to me. What if I had pretended and married him? What would marriage have been like with a man so impatient? A man who loved only on the surface? If he could leave me so easily, how could he have loved me?

Still, he was my first lover, and being abandoned hurts, no matter how much I rationalized it. I had a sinking feeling that kept on sinking lower. Again, there was no one with whom to share my disappointment and pain. I don't remember if I regressed to the ignorance of my childhood or if I applied metaphysical theory. I either told myself that life was something that just happened to me or that this was my karma, that I must have rejected him in a past life for an equally silly reason and hurt him the way he had hurt me.

In retrospect, the experience made the first dent in my glamorizing of romantic relationships. My parents and most couples in the village had unions that were based on economic need. The popular German songs of the '50s were exceptionally sentimental and romantic. I had great expectations of having a man miraculously "save" me without my doing anything except being passive. I was to learn that that was impossible, but in this respect I turned out to be a slow learner.

In 1967-'68 I had a roommate, Erika, from the Black Forest in Germany, who played an important role in my life and would again twenty years later. Although trained as a book restorer, she was employed in a household nearby. She introduced me to something I had not yet been exposed to, namely culture. She understood art and often made trips to the museums in Manhattan. She loved the theater, especially Greek tragedies, and I remember seeing *Iphigenia at Aulis* with her in the Circle in the Square, a theater in Greenwich Village. Irene Papas played the title role, and I was very impressed that she got so into the role and cried real tears for a good part of her performance. Erika also tried her hand at many forms of art: photography, drawing, calligraphy, poetry. She taught me that art was for everybody, not just the elite.

I, on the other hand, introduced her to metaphysics. I talked to her about every topic I found in the Edgar Cayce books: the ancient civilizations of Lemuria and Atlantis, reincarnation, karma, prophesy. We experimented with a vegetarian diet and loved to prepare fresh salads. Toward the end of her stay, we made a three-week Greyhound bus trip to Yellowstone Park and the Grand Canyon. She then suddenly decided to return to Germany. Despite her professional training in book restoring, she chose to take up nursing, as it was a more loving and service-related occupation. She said that if it had not been for me, she would not have made the professional change.

One day as we were talking about metaphysics, I mentioned that I wished there was a school that taught such information in a systematic manner. To my surprise she told me that her mother studied with the Arcane School, a metaphysical correspondence school located in New York City. She thought this school might be right for me.

Shortly thereafter, I applied to the Arcane School and was accepted. The school was founded in 1923 by Alice Bailey, following the publication of the first of eighteen books dictated to her through mental telepathy by Djwhal Khul, a Tibetan lama. Alice Bailey also founded several spiritual service organizations and the Lucis Publishing Company under the overall name of Lucis Trust. All activities (except book sales) are free of charge and maintained by voluntary contributions. Being an Arcane School student meant submitting myself to a threefold discipline: daily meditation, daily spiritual study, and service to humanity in a form of my own choice. The first set of study materials contained passages from *Three Lectures on the Vedanta Philosophy* by Max Müller. His words have been a guiding light to me ever since:

> "Do not believe in what you have heard; do not believe in traditions because they have been handed down for many generations; do not believe in anything because it is rumored and spoken of by many; do not believe merely because the written statements of some old sages are produced; do not believe in conjectures; do not believe in that as truth to which you have become attached by habit; do not believe merely on the authority of your teachers and elders. After observation and analysis, when it agrees with reason and is conducive to the good and benefit of one and all, then accept it and live up to it."

I found the Arcane School very complementary to the A.R.E. as they provided me with differing services. Even though it has no correspondence school, the A.R.E. makes the wisdom of the Cayce readings available to the world. It builds connections among people via workshops, conferences, and study groups. (Using *A Search for God*, Books I and II, as texts, study group members meditate, pray, and discuss spiritual disciplines to apply the Cayce principles more fully in their lives.) The Edgar Cayce teachings speak to my heart and have opened my mind. They have given me knowledge and wisdom in how to live my life from day to day. There is a wealth of information on how to keep the physical body healthy.

If it weren't for the Edgar Cayce readings, I wouldn't have learned to drink lots of water every day and to walk whenever possible to keep myself healthy. I might have gotten onto more psychic byways than highways without his warning to stay away from such practices as the Ouija board. I also learned to set my own ideals and to take control of my mind and of my life. I attended several five-day workshops at the A.R.E. in Virginia Beach, and twice I spent a week at the A.R.E. family camp. These were inspiring and love-filled experiences.

Studying with the Arcane School, on the other hand, is academic and impersonal, and helped to raise my consciousness to the level of abstract, higher mind. I discovered how to differentiate among my physical, emotional, and mental bodies, and learned practices that would help me to integrate them into a unified personality. I learned how to identify soul energy and aspired to have my soul manifest through my unified personality. The Arcane School study also taught me mental discrimination between good and bad, right and wrong, valuable and worthless, illusion and reality, as well as mental disciplines and the value of dispassion and detachment.

Both organizations have enriched my life. It is true that I was not able to share any except the most basic of metaphysical knowledge with my family, but I had found a new family, the universal family of the spirit. Accepting that everyone had lived before, I began to see myself and my family in a new light. I could not expect anyone to be perfect, because everyone has to return to learn more lessons. A proper understanding of reincarnation means that a human soul reincarnates into a human body, unlike the Hindu tradition that maintains we can live in the bodies of animals. The human soul can no more inhabit the body of an animal than a gallon of liquid can be poured into a quart container without overflowing.

Finally, with metaphysical insight, I was able to understand the inequality of human birth. Whether a person was born rich, poor, healthy, sick, loved, or neglected was caused by that person's behavior in past lives. At first I saw the law of karma, or cause and effect, as strictly "an eye for an eye, a tooth for a tooth." I believed that someone like me who had a cruel and abusive mother had been a cruel and abusive mother in another life. This was logical, but to my intuitive mind it was lacking God's divine love.

Eventually, I figured out that the effect in this life of being an abused child could have one of several causes in an earlier life. For instance, I could have been an abused child or an abused adult in a past life and needed to experience abuse again so that I would learn to choose love. Another possibility is that I could have been an abusing mother and needed to experience abuse so that I would learn to love. It is also possible that I could have chosen to experience abuse in order to learn compassion quickly or in order to eventually teach others how to love. Finally, my situation could have been a combination of all of these.

Ultimately, I came to see clearly that the purpose behind karma was not to mete out punishment to people and thereby, it is hoped, to teach us to behave properly. Karma is God's way of teaching us, and it is always loving. The law of cause and effect is true throughout the universe, and there is a reason for everything. Nothing is an accident. God, I discovered, is behind it all. God, finally, was wonderful to me. Discovering this new way of looking at life was a beautiful revelation.

My first promotion at the *Daily News* in 1967 transferred me into the research department, where I worked for two managers. They did not have enough to keep me busy and, when I complained, they said they were powerless and that I should find a way to fill my time. My predecessor had been pregnant and knitted booties, jackets, and hats for her baby, but I brought in metaphysical books and read for several hours every day. My desk was hidden away and only people who intended to walk down the back stairway passed that way. They often stopped and chatted since I had time.

I came across a fascinating metaphysical myth about Hercules in *The Twelve Labors of Hercules*, by Alice Bailey. In the myth, Hercules symbolizes the universal disciple. The information in this myth touched me in a profound and personal way. It revealed to me what one of my problems was and also led me to the solution. In the story, Hercules is sent into a swamp to kill the nine-headed hydra, a kind of snake, which had devastated the countryside and killed many people. Before he could even approach the monster, Hercules had to overcome his fear and revulsion. Then he took his sword and hacked away at its nine heads. Each time he cut off one head, two new ones grew in its place. Thoroughly frustrated, he discovered by accident that when he knelt on the ground and lifted the monster into the air, it lost its power, and he could kill it.

The hydra symbolizes our unconscious mind with its negative desires for sex, comfort, money, and power; its hatred, pride, separateness, and cruelty; and its fears. All of these feelings take us away from God, and they have to be made conscious with practices of discrimination, patience, and humility. Looking at myself, I intuitively understood that the biggest head on my own hydra was fear. The reason that I was a "still water that runs deep" was not only because I was deep, but also because I was afraid to open my mouth and speak my mind. So many terrible things could happen if I spoke up. I could be ridiculed, I could be contradicted, and I could be ignored. In any case I would feel ashamed, stupid, and unimportant, and that was painful.

While walking along the narrow boardwalk by the East River one day, I had a clear insight that what I feared was violence that came from other human beings and was directed at me by their words and gestures. Slowly I became aware of the connection between my fears and the verbal abuse I had suffered as a child. The Arcane School meditation, which I faithfully carried out every morning, was directed at purifying the emotional body and integrating it into the personality. Passages in the Edgar Cayce readings also inspired me. "Criticize not unless ye wish to be criticized." (Edgar Cayce reading 2936-2) The Arcane School taught that the emotions must be handled from above, by the mind, and the mind by the soul. At the time, I expected that my spiritual reading, meditation, and service would result in emotional health and happiness.

Inspired by a young colleague, Michael, who had just graduated from college, I applied to Queens College for the spring 1970 semester and was accepted. I had become an American citizen four years earlier. During the second semester at Queens College, in November of 1970, my father died at the age of sixty. I took two weeks' leave from work and school and flew to Germany for his funeral.

Once I arrived, my mother asked me if I wanted to see my father's body in the coffin, but I chose not to. I needed no proof that he was dead, and I wanted my mind to carry his living image as a sunburned, black-haired vibrant man in his forties. He was actually sixty, but my mental image of him had not aged. My father was buried in the small cemetery outside Köhlen. People from the village whom I had not seen in nearly ten years came and shook my hand while I remained stunned.

This was my third visit since I had left, as I had spent several weeks with my parents in 1967. This time I visited neither relatives nor friends but remained in the house with my mother. She, Kati (also visiting from the States), and I, and sometimes my brothers Richard and Johann as well, played board games for entertainment. My parents had been married thirty-six years and my mother missed my father. In between setting up the board, she confessed how difficult it was for her to get to sleep without him beside her.

"Thirty-six years we slept in the same bed," she said and began to cry. Kati tried to cheer Mother up, but I stopped her.

"Please let her cry. She has to," I said, remembering that I had never seen her cry before, although Tina had told me that she had once entered the barn and discovered Mother sitting on a stool, crying bitterly. Tina had been shocked speechless. She had run into the house, told Papa, and asked him to go to Mother and bring her back into the house, which he did. During that trip home I began to reconnect to my feelings of sadness and grief. From reading Elisabeth Kübler-Ross's book *On Death and Dying*, I knew for certain that it was natural to cry and unhealthy to repress tears. Even though my mother had inflicted pain on me and had prevented me from crying, I was not interested in revenge and wanted to lessen her suffering, if I could. I turned to Mother and said, "It's all right. You can cry whenever you want to, and I'll even cry with you. For a whole year you can cry as much as you want. Anyway, that's what the experts say. After a year it will be time to stop. But until then, you just cry." I actually patted her arm. In her grief, my mother was soft, gentle, and receptive, a side I had never seen in her. For a moment, she was the child and I was the mother. That felt good and released me from seeing her only in the role of cruel mother. She was also a grieving wife, and that fact made me aware of the changability of relationships and the various roles we play in life.

In an effort to understand my mother as a person in her own right, I had been asking question about her childhood and her parents. I knew that she came from a wealthy farming family in a village twenty kilometers from Köhlen and that she had two sisters and one brother. I had also learned that her father and mother valued masculinity above everything in their children. This grandfather, whom I never met, was consequently only interested in his son. My mother and her sisters envied masculinity and imitated men's ways and competed fiercely with each other for their father's approval and love, which they never obtained. My mother had unconsciously carried her father's value system, where gender is concerned, into her marriage and projected it onto her children. I realized she was also a daughter and a sister.

Back in New York, feeling not only the loss of my father's physical existence, but also the loss of what he had represented in my mind, I began to approach the abyss of despair. Even though I had made progress in accepting my feelings and had been able to encourage my mother to express her grief, I had not yet fully learned how to accept or express my feelings and did not know how to process my grief about my father's death.

One day in 1969, Mr. Krieger, the director of the three advertising departments, including research, passed by my desk when I was deeply engrossed in a book. He asked about my work, and I said it was completed. He asked if this happened often, and I said yes. A few weeks later I was promoted to executive secretary, and I intuitively knew it was his doing. Later he told me he thought I was being "wasted" in an easy job. I now worked for one of the advertising managers, Mr. Way. He was short, had been in the navy, and always drank his coffee black. He got his own coffee from the coffee wagon.

Mr. Krieger's office, which was a few doors down, was the corner office since he was the highest executive on the floor. Looking back on it now twenty-four years later, I don't understand how I could have gotten into such a pickle about this man as I did. He was fifty-eight years old, about six feet tall, with broad shoulders. His hair was nearly white, his skin was ruddy, and he had the bushiest white eyebrows I had ever seen. He had a very open, perhaps even young, mind. He was also of German descent and spoke a few words of German.

I still smoked in 1969, so, when he came to see my boss, he would first bum a cigarette from me. "What are you smoking today?" he would ask. "You got one for me? You can have one of mine any time. Just ask." I would offer him a mentholated Newport, and he would light it. Sometimes he offered me one of his in exchange, would take out his matches, and light it for me.

He would also come by to check on how I had done with the "Jumble." The Jumble was a word game that appeared in the *Daily News* every day. The letters of four five-letter words were mixed up, and the reader had to figure out the words. Certain of the letters were circled and they made up the clue to the accompanying cartoon. Often he came by and said: "How did you do with the Jumble today? Did you get the fourth word? I couldn't get it. What is it?" It was fun because he had a positive energy and was always cheerful.

Another thing he would ask was whether I had recently bought a new issue of the German magazine, *Stern*. If I had, I showed it to him. He would put it on my desk, bend over it, leaf through it, and point out things in the advertisements that were done differently from the way we did them at the paper. Sometimes we talked about other items, such as sailing or vacation. But I felt shy. I, the little German country girl, was enormously flattered by the attention this big city executive paid to me. He obviously enjoyed talking with me, and no one else received as much attention from him as I. But what was his attraction toward me?

In retrospect, I think he sincerely liked me. Once he said, "I love your potential." Probably that is all he loved about me and I did not realize it, but as for me, I had developed a crush. I think he intended only to have fun with me, but he did not realize that I would misunderstand. Because of the rejections I had experienced, I was confused, and I did not know it. Those fun and games became intense emotional suffering for me. I had no skill in handling my emotions.

Entries in my journal for that year focus on the director's behavior toward me and my adolescent feelings.

I was elated when Mr. Krieger spent time with me at my desk, looking at the advertisements in a German magazine. I agonized when he did not come around for even a single day. When I was invited to sit next to him on the dais at my boss's retirement luncheon, I was afraid of having a nervous breakdown. At twenty-six, I had regressed to the emotional age of a young girl going through puberty, intuitively knew of my immaturity, and despaired because of it. I wanted to understand what was going on in me, but my reason seemed to hit a brick wall. The retirement party went very well, and I even enjoyed myself. Mr. Krieger smoked my cigarettes throughout and offered me his in return. By now everybody in the department seemed to know that he liked me, but nobody ever made any insinuating remarks that this liking could be personal. I seemed to be the only one who saw a personal connection.

On my weekends during this time, I often drove out to Long Island beaches and took long walks along the ocean, while I tried to process what to do about Mr. Krieger. With friends from India, I visited Mystic Seaport in Connecticut. I spent a one-week vacation in complete solitude in a little house on Heinz's property in the Catskill Mountains. This house was used by hunters in the winter and had no running water and an inner door that did not close properly. Water had to be fetched in a bucket from a well 500 yards away. I felt at home there, and the weather that week was perfect. I lay in the sun or under the apple trees, which were blooming, went for walks in the woods and along the stream. I drove into town for food only twice.

In the evenings I sat alone in the main room and read, meditated, or wrote in my journal. The window shade still had the message I painted on it in large letters during the sixties: "Suppose they gave a war and nobody came." This week turned out to be a respite from my suffering. I wrote down my prayer to the feminine part of God:

Great Mother of the World,
What is the meaning of this?
I have asked you so many times
Sometimes your answer is a smile
Sometimes you say, "Find out for yourself,"
And sometimes you don't even listen.
What is the meaning of this, Great Mother?
Is he like one of the lessons you have sent to me over the years?
Am I to sit in your classroom for another lecture and then walk out and forget the bitter method by which it was taught?
Can you really be so cruel, Great Mother?
Isn't there another way to pull your creatures into heaven?
Let me love him, Great Mother
Let me be what he needs
Let me give him what he wants.
Teach me with beauty, Great Mother, with beauty and truth of this world.

The second week of my vacation I drove to State College, Pennsylvania, and visited "Uncle John" Spotts. He embodied qualities that I seemed to be lacking and that I hoped to build into my personality. I appreciated his common sense, strength, independence, and maturity. In an emotional sense, he was sanity personified. Uncle John lived next door to a church in a little house he had built himself before he married. He loved people, and I had asked him once if he did not want to marry again. He said no; he had had a happy relationship with his wife and did not think a second marriage could be as good. He had a son and daughter-in-law, but no grandchildren. While I visited, he insisted on sleeping in a small attic room and assigned the main bedroom to me. He treated me as if I were the granddaughter he never had. I felt comfortable with him as if I had known him for a very long time.

When I woke up in the morning, I usually found him in the patio reading inspirational literature. He insisted on cooking me breakfast. During the five days I spent with him, we visited his neighbors and friends: the Bohns and the Lightners, who had a hunting lodge deep in the woods, where they invited us for an incredible Sunday brunch plus homemade ice cream. Through "Uncle John" I got a taste of middle-class American families who had been here for generations. He also told me about what he had done when he was in Africa. He had made furniture for the missionaries and wooden incubators for premature babies in the hospital. He confessed, with a smile, that he had eaten alligator meat and liked it. We went for a very long walk through the Pennsylvania woods, going up and down ravines, helping each other over rocks and underneath low-hanging branches. I felt validated as a human being in this relationship that was without pretense and without artifice.

The trips to the Catskills and to State College gave me courage to do something to end my suffering at the office. I told Mr. Krieger how I felt in a letter, which I mailed to his house. "I could love you" was my main message.

A week or so after I sent it, his secretary was out ill, and he called me to fill in for her. We worked well together all day until the late afternoon. During a quiet moment, however, I stepped into the adjacent empty office and stood by the window, looking out. It was early winter and Manhattan was beginning to go dark. He followed me, and I asked, "Did you receive my letter?"

"Yes, I did," he said.

"And?" I asked.

"I cannot" was all he said, and it seemed to me that he sounded sad and compassionate. I don't remember what I responded, but he simply repeated, "I cannot." A tear ran down my cheek. He came close to me and picked it off with his finger. His face was full of pain. Was he participating in my pain, like an empath, or was I seeing his pain? He was a sensitive man, but I did not think that he was feeling my pain as if it were his. If he, too, hurt, I could not understand why.

The emotional content of this scene was replayed numerous times in my dreams in which sometimes he, sometimes I, sometimes both of us, would be crying, yet hiding our pain from each other. Even though my relationship with him had only been platonic, in my dreams I often found myself beside him in a large bed. I could not label these dreams as "wish fulfillment" and came to believe that perhaps he and I had had an intimate relationship in a past life. That would explain the attraction and the caring we felt for each other. I don't believe that he consciously toyed with me, but rather that my presence stirred up feeling in him which, for some reason only he knew, he could not act upon.

The esoteric knowledge in the books that more and more filled up my apartment were of no help with my emotional pain and confusion. Prayer and meditation helped some with the pain, but at that time I still had no idea what a mountain of pain I had repressed since childhood. I despaired about my lack of relationships and about my perception that I was immature. I asked the universe, "What should I do?" But it would be a while before the answer was clear. The Edgar Cayce readings made the point that none of our experiences happens by chance and that each experience is for our growth. In retrospect, one of the roles Mr. Krieger played was to stimulate my feelings so that my emotional repression was beginning to come undone. Emotions held tightly in check for years were bursting to the surface.

Chapter 4
Breakthrough

> Let the body-mind continue in the attitude of seeking for the *spiritual* awakening. Know that each experience in this material plane is, if used in a constructive manner, *for soul development*!
>
> —(Edgar Cayce reading 1445-1)

ONE night in 1972 I sat down at the table in my apartment and calmly considered ending my life. This thought had been in the back of my mind for some time, and again and again I had fearfully pushed it away. It was finally time to face myself, holding this thought and either doing something about it or dismissing it. The thought became a wish, and the wish was to put an end to my unhappy life. How would I end it, though? I looked around the apartment to examine my options. I could close the windows tightly and put wet rags under the door. If I then turned on the gas, late at night, I would probably succeed in snuffing out my life before anybody smelled the gas.

Would Mr. Krieger come to my funeral? Would anyone

else from the office come? Would he feel guilty? My family, would they miss me? Would anybody care? I did not think that anybody would really miss me or feel guilty. Even if Mr. Krieger attended my funeral and felt guilty, what he did was not really important. What I did was important as only my actions would have consequences for me. Yes, I could end my life and my suffering. Growing up in Germany with a cruel mother and a neglectful father had not prepared me to function emotionally as an adult. Even though I had older sisters, I could not expect emotional or mental support from them. I could hold a job, but I failed in intimate love relationships. In spite of my superior intelligence (in 1967 I had taken a Mensa IQ test and scored 129), my emotions caused me nothing but pain.

If I died, I would see Franz-Heinz again, wouldn't I? Would being dead be any fun, though? There would be no kissing, no holding hands, no walking together. What would really happen if I died? If I killed myself? Was there a difference? According to Edgar Cayce, there was. Even in the case of suicide, it made a difference what the motive was. In *Many Mansions* Gina Cerminara describes one woman who committed suicide to escape disgrace and another who did so because she resented being controlled by her husband. The karmic consequence in both cases was loneliness and feeling like a misfit. W.H. Church in his book *Many Happy Returns* writes that Edgar Cayce himself had committed suicide in a life in ancient Troy out of humiliation and rage. For most of his life Cayce had felt subconsciously guilty, but had finally overcome it in patience and love, through forgiveness of self and others. Did I not already feel lonely and like a misfit? The more I thought about suicide, the more familiar the idea felt, as if I had already done it myself once before in another life.

On 27 December 1972 I woke up after midnight from a loud noise made by a truck that stopped suddenly on Jamaica Avenue at the red light. I wanted to fall asleep again quickly, so I purposely breathed slowly and deeply. I was very calm and noticed with detachment that my feet and legs seemed to have risen while my physical legs and feet remained resting on the mattress. I continued the slow breathing. My entire body then seemed to rise up until I actually felt I were in the shoulder stand. I remained there, but stopped the deep and slow breathing and just breathed normally. Slowly my body, what I had come to identify as my "astral" body from my Arcane School studies, sunk down and back into my physical counterpart. Again I breathed deeply and slowly, and once again my feet, legs, and then hips rose up into the shoulder stand.

A second time I breathed normally, and my astral body rejoined my physical body. When I was up in the shoulder stand for the third time, I had the desire to move an arm—but I could not. I was paralyzed. I tried to force myself to move, but I could not. Then I panicked, and it seemed as though my astral body suddenly crumbled, fell down, and reassembled back inside my physical body.

This was not a dream and it was not my imagination. Something unusual had happened. Was it what was called an out-of-body experience or astral projection? I had read that it was possible for the soul to leave the body and enter it again. Although I had not been totally outside, there had been a partial separation. For now, I decided to put my suicide on hold.

As soon as I could, I visited a metaphysical bookstore and bought all the books on the subject that I could find. Muldoon and Carrington, two researchers who had themselves experienced astral projection, seemed the most reliable writers. According to their book, instead of panicking, I should have given myself the suggestion to remain emotionally calm. That would have helped to bring about a conscious projection. I hoped to have another opportunity so that I could try it.

Four nights later, I awoke after a vivid dream about Mr. Krieger. While I lay in bed and reflected on the dream, I became aware of a floating sensation throughout my body. This feeling of energy then seemed to unite and stream toward my feet. It then gathered force there and streamed back toward my head as if it wanted to come out. This happened several times. Somehow I felt calm and fearless through the experience and desired to leave my body.

Just then I remembered reading about a little "as if" trick that might facilitate the separation. I pretended that I was out of the body already and pictured myself standing on top of a Manhattan skyscraper looking down. Immediately below me I saw not the city, but a patch of forest. I was lying prone and floated in the air. I was filled with peace. Below me I could distinctly see mature trees surrounding young evergreen trees. My whole being was occupied with the perception of this scene. Then I became aware that I was not seeing this from any place in the city. Suddenly, the scene shifted.

I now lay on my back in mid-air and was moved with great precision by some force, or intelligence, or intelligent force. I was moving sideways, and threads of light a foot long and electric sparks were shooting from my body, pushing me along.

I sensed, not with my mind but with my entire body, that I had now moved through the solid door back into my apartment. When I reached a position directly over my physical body in the bed, I stopped moving for an instant, then I was moved downward. The electric threads and sparks shot upward. Still not able to see it, I sensed my physical body on the bed below. My astral head was above the physical chest, astral feet extended beyond the physical feet.

I was moved straight down into my body and then forward until my astral body was perfectly aligned inside my physical. My astral consciousness now reunited with my physical. I touched the skin on my left arm—it felt cold and clammy, but I felt good overall and quite excited about what had happened.

Concurrent with this exciting, baffling new experience in my life, there was a major crisis in the New York City newspaper business. The *New York Times*, the *New York News*, and the *New York Post* wanted to automate their papers, but the printers refused to accept automation even though they were promised that no one would be fired; the papers would follow the slow process of attrition. At the *Daily News* six or seven executive secretaries, including myself, were given secret training to operate perforating machines so that we would be able to replace the printers when they struck. For this purpose, we were chauffeured to a secret (and safe) location in New Jersey every day for several weeks to learn and practice. So, while I was fully occupied with the excitement of everyday events at the paper, I made a clear suggestion to my subconscious mind. I gave the instruction that if I ever had another out-of-body experience, I wanted to see my physical body. That would be proof to me that I was actually outside of it. In less than two months, on 23 February 1973, it happened again.

I woke up at 1:15 a.m. and experienced the floating sensation, then the energy moved toward my feet, gathered strength there, and again moved toward my head as if it wanted to come out. After several attempts, I felt tired. Going out of my body seemed so tedious. I gave up wanting. Suddenly the power became a rushing sound in my ears. Separation was smooth and easy. I floated above my body in the air, lying on my left side, my right hand under my head, in exactly the same position as I had lain in bed. I was filled with peace and serenity and felt free from all negative feelings.

Then my mind told me that I had asked it to remind me

to look for my physical body. I wished to see it, and instantly I saw before me the Murphy bed door. I did not have to open my eyes—the desire alone gave me vision. I sensed the distance to the bed below: a little more than one yard. I turned my head downward and saw my head and shoulders on the pillow.

My face looked strangely round and curved—more like my sister's face than my own, which I had never seen in relief, but only flat in mirrors and photographs. I felt detached from my body in the bed, had no feelings for it, and observed it impersonally and with curiosity. But my body exerted a magnetic pull on me, and I knew that if I continued to look at it, it would draw me back. I wanted to continue to feel the peace and the serenity and not the negative emotions which seemed to belong to the physical body.

I turned my head and slowly rose higher and nearly touched the ceiling. Inches from my face was the narrow upper surface of the Murphy bed door. Recently I had painted the door a bright yellow and now saw that the surface had splatters of yellow paint and was covered by a thin layer of dust. I perceived the conditions directly, without thought and without distortion. Then the power moved me gently down and lowered me into the physical body. For a moment I was aware of darkness, until I opened my eyes, and this time I had to use a small amount of physical energy to lift my eyelids.

Several things became clear to me. First, I was not my body, but that which lived in it. My soul and mind could be outside my physical body and could return to it. When my body eventually died or if I killed it, *I* would most likely not die with it, but still exist in consciousness.

I thought that it was one thing to read about the existence of the soul in books, but quite another to find myself outside my body, to exist as pure consciousness, with my mind sort of looking on over my shoulder and reminding me that I want to see the body, my own body, in front of me. I felt an intense gratitude that I was able to experience the reality of the soul and the body and see so clearly that both existed. With this experience, I again felt that something extraordinarily beautiful and precious was within me and flowed into every part of me, my mind, my feelings. This preciousness had glimmered for the first time years ago when Herr Koop had tutored me in pronouncing the philosophical poem. Meanwhile, I had learned from my metaphysical studies that we all have an eternal soul which, more precious than the body, is birthless and deathless.

The day after this last experience, the secretaries had once again been chauffeured to New Jersey to work on the perforating machines. Three secretaries and two of the men who were teaching us were sitting around a small table and eating our lunch. I remember eating a grilled cheese-and-tomato sandwich. Because I was not in the city and the work situation was so unusual, I mentioned the very strange experience I'd had the night before. I described it in a few words. No one laughed. No one ridiculed me. Several people had heard of such experiences, although no one else had experienced them.

The printers called a strike at all three newspapers. At the *Daily News* our operation was installed next to the executive dining room, behind steel doors, and armed guards were stationed outside the door. It was feared that the printers might do something, like throw a bomb, to paralyze our operation. We had lunch every day in the executive dining room. Once I sat next to the president of the paper, Tex James. At another time during dinner after working very late, I mentioned the long subway ride I had to take to get home. A man at the opposite side of the table offered to give me the money for a taxi. I felt I could not accept it and said flippantly, "I don't even know you." To my embarrassment, a colleague beside me whispered, "He is the treasurer; you can accept it."

After three weeks of extra hard work and lunch and dinner in the executive dining room, the printers finally ended their strike. Work was back to normal. I reflected more on the astral projection I had experienced. Committing suicide was out of the question to me now. Somewhere I had read that if individuals commit suicide, whatever the problem is they are running away from, it will be waiting for them when they reincarnate. It would be silly to run away from something that follows you. Somehow, this out-of-body experience convinced me that the thing to do was to confront it.

I marveled at the state of consciousness I had experienced while outside my body. I was *pure* consciousness. I perceived directly, needing neither senses nor reason. My mind was like a servant that did my bidding as I had trained it. I was not the body. I was not the senses. I was not the mind. I was the consciousness that gave life to the mind, the senses, and the body. There was another, an even higher, part which had willed the experience and had moved me through space. I believe this part was an impersonal will, intelligence, and love. I believe that I had contacted God within me. Many years later I would come face to face with this higher part, personified and assuming my own face, albeit in perfection.

Pondering these out-of-body experiences, I received a strong intuitive impression that they were connected to an act of suicide in a past life. It further seemed to me that the divinity within had given me these out-of-body experiences to reveal to me the immortality of the self or soul, so that I would not make the mistake of suicide a second time. I saw this as an experience of pure grace. I thought that it was possible that I had earned this gift in a past life through some kind of exemplary loving behavior.

I rarely mentioned the out-of-body experiences to anyone. I was, however, a member of the American Society for Psychical Research (ASPR) and learned that the Society collected reports of out-of-body experiences. I filled in their six-page questionnaire and mailed it back. The thank-you letter from the ASPR included the sentence: "You have very good insight into your experiences," which pleased that part of me that was doubting my sanity.

After several semesters at Queens College, I switched to The New School for Social Research, a private university located in Greenwich Village in Manhattan. In a creative writing course with Professor Freeman I chose innocent and safe topics: how to raise African violets, how one of my kittens dominated the other one, etc. When I wrote a paper on my out-of-body experiences, wondering if the professor would approve or ridicule me, he wrote the following on the returned paper:

> Why haven't you written about his before? Kittens are appealing and provide useful writing practice, but when you have a message of this magnitude and a ready-made audience, how can you resist for so long? . . . My only complaint is that you didn't make more of an effort to integrate these experiences for the reader. How do you explain this? What do you think it means? How do other projectors view this kind of experience? What do traditional scientists have to say about this, if anything?

The doctrine of reincarnation teaches that the soul enters the body at or before birth and leaves it at death, but it is not generally known that it may leave the body for short periods during life. Edgar Cayce indicated in his readings that the soul frequently leaves the body during sleep. In reading 853-8 he was asked for specifics:

> *(Q) Do I actually leave my body at times, as has been indicated, and go to different places?*
>
> (A) You do.
>
> *(Q) For what purpose, and how can I develop and use this power constructively?*
>
> (A) Just as has been given as to how to enter into meditation. Each and every soul leaves the body as it rests in sleep . . . Study to show thyself approved unto God, a workman not ashamed of that you think, of that you do, or of your acts; keeping self unspotted from your own consciousness of your ideal; having the courage to dare to do that you know is in keeping with God's will.

I had no further out-of-body experiences but remained fascinated by accounts of them and read what I could about the subject. The second part of Muldoon's book, *The Case for Astral Projection,* contains dozens of firsthand accounts from individuals all over the world who experienced astral projection, sometimes during sleep or while nearly dying from an accident or an illness or while under the influence of anesthesia in a hospital operating room.

I was now thirty years old. The out-of-body experiences, although they kept me from ending my life, had for a time diverted me from my emotional difficulties. Prayer and meditation clearly was not enough. In the fall of 1973 I got ready for work one morning, brushed my hair, and accidentally damaged the ligaments around two discs in my spine. I spent twelve days in the hospital in traction with heavy weights dangling from the foot of my bed. I learned that people who usually get the injuries I had received them while lifting heavy objects. All I had lifted were my heavy emotions.

I had begun writing down my dreams in 1970, following Edgar Cayce's advice. If someone said that he or she had no dreams, Cayce would remark that that individual was too "lazy" to remember them. " . . . all visions and dreams are given for the benefit of the individual, would they but interpret them correctly . . . the reflection . . . of the subconscious . . . or a projection from the spiritual forces to the . . . individual . . . " (Edgar Cayce reading 294-15) In the very first dream that I wrote down I observed a group of happy deer jumping through a forest clearing and talking to each other. A forest ranger, who also watched them, warned me not to talk about them to people in the city, as they would not understand. I believed the deer represented my intuitive and psychic sensitivities, and people in the city referred to people with minds that were closed to such matters.

My failed relationships, my out-of-body experiences, my obsession with the advertising director, and my sadness made me ask the same question my angry and frustrated mother had hurled at me so often: "Have you gone completely mad?" Was I emotionally sick or mentally unbalanced? A dream that came in 1973 has been truly a gift and an inspiration. It seemed to indicate that, if I was not healthy and whole on the outside, I was so in the very core of my being.

I dreamed that I stood on a path in a forest with other people. I saw a tree nearby, tall and beautiful. I lifted my head back and looked at it. It towered above the other trees and was very strong and healthy. The foliage was full and bright green. Among the leaves was an abundance of white blossoms that grew in triangular bunches with the tips pointing upward, like chestnut blossoms. The sky above the tree was a clear blue.

Elsie Sechrist, a student and colleague of Edgar Cayce's, states in her book *Dreams, Your Magic Mirror* that trees are often symbols of our own spiritual state; that if they look healthy, we are enjoying individual growth; when they are dying through neglect or for lack of water, we must search within ourselves for our spiritual deficiencies. She says that the triangle represents a human being's experience in the earth, and if it is set within a circle, it represents the dreamer's union with the divine self. Green, the color of the leaves, is, of course, the color of the heart chakra, as well as the color of healing and of growth. White, the color of the blossoms, represents purity.

After I recovered from what I termed my "psychological" back injury, I decided to explore psychotherapy to see if that could be of help. My out-of-body experiences had certainly done the job of dissuading me from suicide, but the despair that had pushed me toward suicide had not abated. Yes, I felt some relief and felt closer to God, but I was still unhappy. I did not know what the problem was. I found a therapist and made an appointment one evening after work. While parking my car outside his office, I hit a fire hydrant and dented my fender. It was the first time in five years of driving that I hit anything. I think I was nervous and scared.

Dr. Ross was a man in his early forties. I sat in a chair with my back to the wall and his desk was to my right. He sat behind it and asked me questions. No matter what he asked me, I cried. I did not know why I cried, and I could not stop. He did not think crying was helpful, and after four weeks said, "I don't think I am helping you. All you do is sit here and cry. I know a good doctor in Manhattan, and I recommend that you see him."

That doctor was Dr. Albert Ellis, who was famous for his book *Guide to Rational Living* and is known as the founder of rational-emotive therapy. In April of 1974 I had my first appointment with him. In the beginning I saw him privately. Usually I sat nervously on the leather couch in his lavish study while he relaxed on a black leather recliner, seeming slightly bored. Later, I joined a therapy group and saw him privately only occasionally.

In his rational-emotive therapy he taught that our negative, irrational thoughts create our negative emotions; by changing our irrational thoughts to logical thinking, we can change our negative and painful emotions. I liked the process because it suited my rational and logical German mind. For months I gained insights into my irrational ways of seeing the world around me and learned to open my mind to other, saner, and kinder possibilities.

With one exception, I did not cry when having sessions with Dr. Ellis. However, halfway through a Saturday group therapy marathon, I began to cry and could not stop the flow of tears. Again, I did not know why I was crying. I asked him, and he had no answer for me either. I thought he should know, theoretically, why a person can cry for hours and not know why. (Later, I learned that when repression is undone, it can cause sudden releases of feelings and tears.) My repression was major, my irrationality was minor, but he did not see that.

I worked with Dr. Ellis for about a year. Then, during a private session, I told him about my out-of-body experiences in 1972. He leaned back in his leather chair, raised his chin into the air, and with a kind of superior smirk told me flat out that there was no such thing. "That was a hallucination," he said and smiled.

I feel fortunate that my studies of the Edgar Cayce readings and my Arcane School work had given me faith in a larger universe than the scientific one and in my own perceptions. The famous psychotherapist's declaration made no dent in my conviction that I had been outside my body. I recalled the admonition in the first Arcane School study set: " . . . do not believe merely on the authority of your teachers and elders." Dr. Ellis was a learned man, but I trusted my perceptions more than his judgment.

In retrospect, I was grateful to Dr. Ellis for everything I had learned from him. What I appreciated most was that he had encouraged his clients never to use the word *should.*

"Every *should*," he said, "is a four-letter word. You must never 'should' on yourself." This was important to me because many of my thoughts were that I "should" do this or that and left out of consideration what I *wanted* to do. Then, if I did not do what I thought I should, I would feel guilty. I had at least finally learned that my "I want" had far more power, more love, and more honesty than any of my "I shoulds."

Chapter 5
Pictures from the Past

I could well imagine that I might have lived in former centuries and there encountered questions I was not yet able to answer; that I had to be born again because I had not fulfilled the task that was given to me.

—(From: *Memories, Dreams, Reflections,* by C.G. Jung)

IN 1975 I moved into a little apartment in Manhattan. While my furniture traveled in a van, I took the Long Island Railroad and a taxi, carrying my parakeets in their cage by hand. I was greeted by Jimmy, a people-loving Irishman and typically friendly and helpful New York City doorman. The building had fourteen floors; my apartment, a bright, cheerful studio facing south with a large bay window, was on the ninth floor. I bought a rug with a Native American pattern in dark red and gold and invested in bookcases of raw wood that I stained and varnished. The parakeets got installed near the window and often sang so noisily that neighbors I met in the hall commented on their cheerful sounds.

I now lived only a few blocks from my office at the newspaper and often came home for lunch, but I was to enjoy the closeness for only about a year. As executive secretary, I had reached the top of the support staff category after only four years of employment. I could no longer be promoted, and I was frustrated. By 1976, after eleven years at the newspaper, I had made two lateral moves, and the second one was a mistake. The woman who had vacated the spot warned me about the executive with whom I would be working. "Don't do it," she said. "He keeps losing things, and it'll always be your fault." I did not listen, but I should have.

She was right. This man was impossible to please. I could not be subservient to such meanness, niggardliness, and empty accusations. Neither could I make another lateral move. I discussed the situation with an executive in the personnel department. We worked it out so that I would resign and receive a nice severance payment. This enabled me to study full-time and fulfill a dream dating back to my first year in the States when Jerry, the son of immigrant parents who were restaurant partners with my sister and her husband, had left to study at Dayton University. I had envied him the pleasure of having four years to do nothing but study. I could now afford—not four years, but at least one year—that same pleasure: the luxury of studying. I signed up for five more courses at The New School for Social Research.

Outside the corporate world I felt freer to be myself, and I maintained a surprisingly busy social life while I studied. I befriended classmates and met them for coffee and dinner. There was Mark, a blond, sensitive, soft-featured artist with a master's degree in English, whom I met at the library. He had spent three years in Japan, lived on the beach while he taught English to Japanese students. One night he brought Japanese paper, ink, and brushes, laid down on the golden carpet in my apartment, and painted tree branches with leaves and singing birds.

Mark introduced me to Sam, who was nearly sixty, masculine yet gentle, and wore a dark mustache. Sam was a writer who worked out of a loft on Seventh Avenue. He was a native New Yorker and unusual in that he was very much an individual. Mark had told me that Sam was looking for someone to work for him part-time. So, I called him and made an appointment. On the appointed day I climbed the two flights to his loft. Sam opened the door and invited me in. Then he sat down and picked up his pipe. I had never been in a New York loft before and looked around surreptitiously as we talked. Sam noticed my curiosity, stopped the conversation, and said, "Feel free to look around. Go ahead. You can look at everything."

So I did. The books on his shelves were different from mine; they seemed so sophisticated. A few of them had his name on them as author. I was in awe. He was the first writer I had ever met. I noticed books about radio programs and mementos from a radio show that he had done about automobiles. I saw a large table with pages from the manuscript on which he was working. There were two typewriters, one had a roll attached that fed paper into it. By the window stood large potted plants. "Well, do you like it?" asked Sam, and I realized he had been watching me. I was overwhelmed with impressions from the place and the person who occupied it. This world was not like the corporate world. Here was freedom, creativity, gentleness. We discussed the work he needed done and that I would come in on Saturday mornings and type his correspondence.

The next Saturday I sat behind one of the typewriters and put one sheet of stationery after another into the machine and typed his letters. Sam sat at the table and edited long sheets of paper that came off the roll. It was quiet in the loft. Finally I handed him the letters and he read them. I was mortified when he discovered that I had misspelled his last name on every single one. He got angry, but did not direct his anger at me. He was safe to be with. He signed the letters anyway, correcting his name with ink.

Sam seemed happy with himself and the world. He took his time to do things and did them thoroughly. He was frugal and wasted nothing. The second Saturday he noticed that I was tense, and he came over, stood behind me, and rubbed my shoulders. He thought for himself and did not care if anyone disagreed with him. In his gentleness and contentment, he reminded me of my father and "Uncle John" Spotts. I spent many Saturdays working with him in his loft, and we became friends.

Neither Dr. Ross nor Dr. Ellis ever inquired about my relationships with my parents. After I had arrived in New York, my mother had answered the long letters I wrote with short notes. I rationalized that she had four, and later six, other children to write to in the States. In her notes she told me negative events that had occurred, bad weather, things that had happened too late, machines that broke or malfunctioned, people who were sick or died. In the first years I sent money and tried to cheer her up; she appreciated the money, but not the cheering up; it "didn't work." Eventually I dreaded opening her letters because they contained bad news and criticism of my positive energy.

At this time I still thought that I had had a normal childhood and a normal mother. I was grateful that my parents were decent, hardworking people who had taught me honesty and respect. In a way I loved my mother; but I also pretended that she had never hurt me and, if so, only because she loved me. I actually thought my shyness and my inferiority complex were without a cause. I saw them as personal defects for which somehow no one was responsible. A dream on 10 May 1975 awakened me rudely to the emotional reality of my relationship with her.

In the dream, I was alone with my mother in a room, and she stood before me and faced me and said: "Kati and Bertha thought they were the first and second in my affections and that you were third, but they were wrong. I didn't care for you at all." I replied, "I knew it, I knew it all along. It was very difficult growing up knowing my mother didn't care for me," and I cried. She opened her arms and wanted to embrace and comfort me. I felt that her compassion was sincere. I also had a distinct feeling of something fatalistic in her not loving me and that she was not to be blamed.

The dream disturbed me. Your mother is supposed to love you. If she doesn't, you are supposed to at least pretend that she does. If you don't want to pretend, you follow modern psychological thought and blame her for her lack of love. Or, if you are the sacrificing type, you assume responsibility and tell yourself that it is all your own fault. It is scary to honestly look your experience in the eye when it goes against the prevailing cultural norms or beliefs. This dream did not indicate that mothers are supposed to love their daughters nor that I was supposed to pretend that she did, but it said something interesting about responsibility or blame. To me it said her lack of love for me was fate, that it was beyond her control to love me.

Through an advertisement in *New York Magazine*, I found a new therapist, Peter. The ad stated that he practiced Transactional Analysis and Gestalt therapy. Peter was only twenty-eight years old and just beginning to set out on his own. He interviewed me about my life and asked many questions about my childhood. My answers seemed to mean more to him than they did to me. At the end, he walked me to the door, musing. Gently, as if he were speaking to a hurt child, he said, "Did you know that your parents emotionally blackmailed you?" I shook my head, "No." I'd had no idea. Dr. Ellis had never inquired about my parents or my childhood, but had only been interested in my present thought processes. What Peter said was a revelation, although I did not quite see how my parents had done that.

During the next two years of weekly group therapy sessions I learned how my behavior and my feelings had been manipulated with threats, insults, and accusations.

Peter held weekly group sessions in the living room of his apartment on a quiet street in Greenwich Village, just below Washington Square Park and New York University. It was a small group, never more than seven or eight people. He had an easel with a large pad of paper standing in the corner of the room, and here he diagrammed our speech according to Eric Berne, the founder of Transactional Analysis. He taught us that the personality consists of three ego states—parent, adult, and child—which roughly correspond to Freud's superego, ego, and id. He drew two figures on the large paper on the easel, each figure consisting of three circles: parent above, adult in the middle, and child below. He explained that any statement made by one person to another could be diagrammed on the paper. Usually we talked about parent-to-child transactions. A parent could make a statement from any of his or her three ego states and could address any of the three ego states of the child.

"Healthy people," said Peter, "make transactions from their adult ego state to the adult ego state of whoever they are speaking to, including parents speaking to their children." Adult-to-adult entails respect for the other and recognition of boundaries. Parent-to-child transactions entail caring, protecting, and mothering. I learned that there was a secondary parent ego state in certain adults; it was called the "pig parent" ego state. This ego state was neither caring nor protecting, but uncaring, insulting, threatening, and accusing.

The child ego state entailed transactions that asked for directions, help, or nurturing. There was also a secondary child ego state called the "adapted child." Because a parent with a "pig parent" would not tolerate a natural child ego state, such a child developed an "adapted child" ego state.

Peter explained that the natural child ego state was the one we needed to rediscover because here lie our natural feelings, desires, and creativity.

I saw that many of my mother's transactions with me—such as, "You know nothing," "Get lost," and "Nobody wants you"—had come from her "pig parent." Her transactions had not been directed to my natural child ego state, but to an artificial me, the adapted child, which did not really exist, but had come into being as a result of being addressed. My mother had communicated to me in ways that confused and paralyzed me, and my natural child went into hiding. She had assaulted me with anger and caused me fear and shock that still affected my communications and my relationships. I made it my goal to work with Peter to understand the dynamics between me and my mother.

Peter stated that, through a child's interactions with others, the adult ego state develops. In a healthy person, all three ego states form a partnership. The parent protects, cares, and nurtures; the adult is the timekeeper and the responsible one; and the child is carefree, spontaneous, feels, and is the creative partner. With my metaphysical background I understood that the soul is in the natural child ego state. So, my second goal was to find the natural child, to make her feel safe, and to let her grow and express herself.

Up to this point in my life, I had found my feelings and emotions to be a hindrance to happiness. To have feelings meant to be in pain. I had been taught to repress all feelings, even injury, and I was very successful in doing that. I lived in my head, thinking, and my behavior was based solely on my thoughts. I was in the masculine mode of living from the intellect and denied my feelings, my fear, anger, as well as my desires. The two phrases I would hear from Peter over and over again were, "What do you feel?" and "What do you want?" Both registered deeply in my consciousness, partly because they confirmed what Edgar

Cayce had said: "[Desire] is the basis of evolution, and of life, and of truth. It also takes hold on hell and paves the way for many that find themselves oft therein. In spirit, in body, in mind." (Edgar Cayce reading 262-60) These two phrases also paved the way for deeper understanding of the prayer, "Father, let Thy desires be my desires. Let my desires, God, be Thy desires, in spirit and in truth." (Edgar Cayce reading 262-60)

Peter had a unique way of working that was more than mere dialogue. During the group sessions, he enabled me to access my repressed feelings and explore my various states of consciousness. I would bring up a present problem, and Peter would help me trace it to its origin in my childhood. He would have me close my eyes, and I often returned to that place of fear and powerlessness in my psyche when I was three or four years old and alone with my mother in the kitchen. Under his guidance I reexperienced her angry yelling, insults, and threats. Peter talked me through it, made me talk back to her, and got me to a place in my psyche where I was in touch with my own power and worthiness. When I opened my eyes, I felt strong and refreshed. It always seemed as if someone had just turned on the lights in the room; it seemed so much brighter than before.

Because of my mother's attitude and behavior toward me, I grew up out of touch with my needs and desires, with the mental habits of rejecting and denying, taking care of others and hoping they would take care of me, feeling disappointed with others when they did not, cruelly blaming myself and consequently feeling guilty, doubting my feelings and opinions, with many resentments and distrust for authority figures, with endless self-doubts and intense feelings of inferiority. Because I had learned to deny my pain and inadequacies and because I was exceptionally bright, I gave others the impression that I was competent and happy.

In 1969, my eighteen-year-old sister Tina had immigrated to the States and settled down in Queens, not far from where I lived. For a while I took on the role of second mother, but we were also friends. We had identical haircuts, and people often took us for twins and confused one with the other. We trusted each other implicitly and supported each other emotionally. My other sisters often criticized or showed the same kind of neglect my mother had shown. Tina and I praised each other's accomplishments in horseback riding, swimming, and other activities we engaged in together.

She was the only one of my brothers and sisters to whom I freely spoke about my childhood memories. She loved and respected me, never doubting my experience. Her experience had been different, and I respected her reality. She was shocked when I told her of Mother's threats, such as to abandon me in a strange place, to sell me to the gypsies, to drown me like an unwanted kitten, or to slaughter me like a pig. Facing her own resistance at first, she then recalled that when Mother was angry, she made cruel threats. I told her that I had felt her anger aimed at me with a destructive purpose and had often felt pierced by it. Tina, however, said that she never felt herself to be the recipient of Mother's anger.

She told me how kind Mother had been when, at the age of thirteen in 1963, Tina had been hospitalized for eight months with a kidney problem. Mother had traveled to Bremerhaven by bicycle and train twice a week and had brought her any delicacy she had requested. I found this interesting and puzzling. Even more interesting was that Tina complained about Papa striking her unjustly for something someone else had done without asking for the facts. We both agreed to a paradox—we had the same parents, but my mother was not her mother, and my father was not her father.

On 4 September 1976, I had an important dream. I dreamed that I was in a kitchen similar to my mother's and she was there with me. I looked out the window and saw a lovely white swan on the meadow. I said to my mother, "Look at that bird, Mother. Hurry up before it goes away." It was so very beautiful, graceful, and elegant. She looked up quickly but immediately returned to her cooking. The swan gracefully walked into the kitchen and stood before me. I stroked its lovely feathered back with my hand. The swan then lifted its head, and I caressed its neck and breast. I felt that this was a special moment full of magic and wonder, and I felt awe that this beautiful animal came so close to me.

According to Elsie Sechrist, author of *Dreams, Your Magic Mirror*, the swan is a symbol of graciousness and beauty. To G.A. Gaskell, author of *Dictionary of All Scriptures and Myths*, the white swan is a symbol of the Higher Self or the individuality. Alice Bailey refers to "the bird or swan out of time and space" and its close connection with wisdom and, therefore, with the psychic nature of God, of humans, and of devas. I took the swan as a symbol for the gracious and beautiful Higher Self, which I was able to see and appreciate, but in which my mother or the mother-part in me was not interested.

During my months in therapy with Peter I trained my mind to revive my forgotten memories of past experiences in my childhood. So, in a way, it was not at all surprising that one day my mind would astound me with a memory of an event that had preceded this life. It happened on a yellow-golden Saturday morning in early November of 1976. As I did my weekly shopping, I found the sidewalk on 35th Street littered with yellow leaves from the London plane trees. When I returned home, I cleaned the apartment, including the bird cage. I was caught up with homework for school and could relax. Sitting sideways on my couch, I leaned against the back rest and brought one foot up. With my eyes open, suddenly I saw vivid pictures in my mind as if someone were showing me a movie in my head.

First, I saw a one-room, stone house unlike any house I had ever seen, standing on the eastern slope of a high mountain. On the other side of the mountain was the Pacific Ocean. I knew that this mountain was part of the Andes and that the continent was South America. The house I looked at was made of one-foot-square gray stone blocks. Inside the house was a young girl, perhaps thirteen or fourteen years old. She was lovely, innocent, and pure, but agitated, confused, and angry. She existed out there in the house in the Andes, but she also existed in my heart and mind.

She was alone in this house on the mountain, with only a guard outside, while her people were in the valley. Her people whom she loved very much. Other girls as pure and innocent as herself, and women, clean and pure in spirit, who gave of themselves as mothers to raise the young girls. All lived in the temple and the women taught the girls proper worship. Every morning they bowed to the new light: "I worship the sun who gives me life, I love the sun as I love my life . . . " Singing was a daily part of life in the temple. So was weaving and playing the flute.

They lived together happily until she was chosen as the best among them, the purest, most virtuous, most accomplished in their arts. Being chosen was supposed to be an honor, but it was no honor to her. She wanted to live, become a teacher like her caretakers or to marry. She used to have a choice, but not any more. How could they let it happen? She puzzled. She agonized. She wondered why the women and her friends were not here to rescue her, to take her back to the temple. "I don't want to die, I want to live . . . " What am I doing? I thought suddenly. What a masochistic fantasy am I having? I don't want this, and I abruptly closed my mind and stopped the pictures and feelings.

According to the journal entry I made that day, I knew I had seen a past life and not some masochistic fantasy. I had only called it that because I was afraid. Initially I did nothing about the experience because I didn't know what to do. Peter was not the person to share it with—he was rational and inexperienced and not a metaphysician. Two weeks passed. Another Saturday. Another lovely and peaceful autumn day. Once again, I sat on the couch in a freshly cleaned and cheerful apartment with all my chores done. Suddenly the door in my mind that I had so abruptly closed two weeks earlier stood wide open again. Once again I saw the house in the Andes with an agitated young girl inside. I decided to see all that would emerge.

The young girl, I learned, was an Incan maiden, and her father was a high official at the court of the Incan emperor. There was peace in the land, and there was no connection yet with Europe. The girl's mother had died when she was about two years old. Her father could not rear her by himself and gave her to the Temple of the Sun. She grew up happy in a loving environment. In particular, I saw a large, very simple hall with a stone floor and stone columns. Many young girls and women who had dedicated their lives to worshiping in the temple lived in this complex. Part of worshiping was weaving, singing, and flute playing. Every year the Inca people chose one of the maidens, called Virgins of the Sun, to be sacrificed for the people. It was kept from the girls, or they denied it, because it came as a tremendous shock to her when she was chosen.

She was brought into the house on the mountain for purification. For how long, I don't know. My feeling was at least three weeks, maybe as long as three months. She was supposed to die without anger or resentment, pure in heart and soul. A young priest walked up the mountain regularly to talk with her and to prepare her for death. He taught her not to be afraid because death was an illusion. He said that she would live again. He influenced her beliefs and convinced her, but he was not able to do anything about her disappointment and anger with the women in the temple.

She spent many sleepless nights in the house on the mountain with only an old soldier sitting watch outside, protecting and guarding her. She often stood by the window at night, which was missing a stone in the wall, and looked down into the moonlit valley, where she knew her people lived and would continue to live while she died. Pain and bitterness filled her heart. How could they let her die when she wanted to live? When she complained to the priest about her sleepless nights, he told her to dance. So, in the middle of the night in a dark room, she danced sometimes until her heart stopped aching and she was tired enough to sleep.

Once, her father and one or two other relatives came to say good-by. Her father was a very proper official who did not show love. In the temple she had only known love, so she threw a temper tantrum.

"I don't want to die!" she screamed. "Do something to save me! I want to live!"

"I can do nothing," he replied stiffly. "It is the law that you must die."

"Then change the law," she screamed.

The father, a true patriarch in an ancient patriarchy, haughtily raised his chin and said, "Not even the emperor can change the law."

Later, one friend said to me, "Oh, but how did you die? I hear that they ripped out the hearts of their victims." I did not know, and I felt no trauma around the actual death. But I became curious and reentered the psychic space purposely. I saw that she had been given a drug and was being carried on a litter down into the valley on a special holiday. She sat up on the litter, barely conscious. Her people celebrated the holiday—and her sacrifice and death. I saw her being carried into a throng of rejoicing people, but I did not see how she died, whether by violence or whether the drug alone ended her life. At the moment of her death, I saw a fleeting image of her soul leaving the confines of her body and flying toward the woods like a swift bird. There had been no pain in dying.

At the time, I had a distinct impression that Peter had been the priest and that Sam had been my father. One Saturday while taking a break from working with Sam in his loft, I surprised him by asking playfully with mock seriousness, "So, Sam, who are you really?" I guess part of me thought it would be grand if Sam revealed to me that he was really a widowed officer at the court of an Incan emperor and had been my father and had grieved over my sacrifice and had met me in this life to heal our relationship. But no such luck. Sam reacted to my playfulness with surprise and said brusquely, "What do you mean, who am I really? You know who I am. I'm Sam!" When I explained why I had asked and told him of my vision, Sam said he did not remember being in Peru as an Incan or as my father, but he sometimes saw pictures in his mind of being in a desert, and he could not explain them since he had never seen a desert in his life.

How did I know this was a vision from a past lifetime? I listed the possibilities of what it could have been and used the process of elimination. It was not a memory from this life because I had never seen such a house in this lifetime. It was also not a dream because dreams happen when you are asleep. I had been fully awake.

It was not a daydream, either. I just never daydreamed. A colleague had recently described to me her daydreams as a process by which she escaped from an unpleasant reality by inventing in her mind a pleasant reality. My vision was not pleasant, and I had not invented it. It had been fully formed in my mind and had become revealed to me.

Since I smoked no marijuana, took no LSD, nor had drunk any alcohol, I could also eliminate a drug-induced hallucination. Could it have been a memory of a movie I had seen on television? No, because not only did I identify with the Incan girl, she was in me and was a part of me. All her feelings were my feelings. Her problems were my problems.

Finally, it also was not what Jungians call an active imagination. A person doing active imagination has numerous choices as to what he or she wants to imagine. I had had no such choice. The vision was fully formed before I became aware of it.

At a conference at the A.R.E. in Virginia Beach on past lives (more about this later), I learned that evidence of our past lives is present in our lives today. If we look for it, we will find it. As I thought about it, I discovered several interesting aspects of my present life that seemed to support this.

First was my love for playing the recorder. Five years before, I went to a music shop and bought a recorder, a wooden flute. Following written instructions, I learned the notes and now play the instrument fairly well for my own enjoyment. I believe my love of this instrument comes from the life in Peru. Wooden flutes, especially pan pipes, are native instruments of the Andean cultures.

The second reason was that I had two or three dreams about llamas and vicuñas. In the dreams, I knew the animals not just intellectually, but familiarly, and cared for them. These animals are native to the Peruvian area, and the Incas domesticated them. Why would a person who grew up in Germany with oxen and cows and who now lives in New York City dream of such unusual animals? Except on television and perhaps in a zoo, I had never seen llamas or vicuñas in this life. I believe that in the Incan life I must have had contact with llamas and vicuñas and come to love them.

Thirdly, I had strong emotional reactions to pictures of Incan ruins. Shortly after I met my friend, Deirdre, she invited me over to her apartment in the West Village to view slides of her visit to Peru. Holding a cup of hot herbal tea, I sat in a deep soft chair in her living room while she put one slide after another on a big white screen in front of us. The Andean Mountains. Houses and temples made with the same gray stone blocks I had seen in my vision. Terraced fields. Stone stairs. Llamas and vicuñas. There were close-ups and long shots, and again and again my inner feelings spoke: "I know this. This is familiar to me. I have lived there. I love that. I miss it. That was my home."

The fourth item was imaging God as the Sun. My relationship with God as a heavenly Father had not been a very easy one, as I was taught that God is an old man with a beard who sits in heaven and watches for children to do something wrong so He can punish them. However, when I asked my mind to give me a picture of God, I saw an image of the golden Sun, giver of life to all in the universe.

At this point, I reexamined my beliefs about reality. I could not agree with my mother that I was crazy, nor with Albert Ellis that I had hallucinated. My out-of-body-experience and this vision of a past life must have been real. They fit in with the theory of an eternal soul and its necessity for repeated incarnations in a human body in order to become perfect. The Edgar Cayce readings, Alice Bailey, and many other sources confirm that such experiences were possible.

Without the insights of Cayce and Bailey and left with my own experiences, my confusion would probably have increased. I might have repressed the experiences so well that I would not even have remembered them. The fear of being thought crazy by others would have made them easy to repress. But because I was familiar with literature about such experiences, I could not discount them. For me, reincarnation became a fact. I was convinced that, as Edgar Cayce had said, life is a meaningful experience, and these experiences had added meaning to my life.

I felt blessed to have had this vision of the Incan maiden. I felt strongly that it was no accident. I had by now established a relationship with the light within that I called the soul. I was sure the vision had been given to me from my soul for a particular purpose. The Incan maiden was a real presence in my personality. Her strong desire to live stood in stark contrast to my ambivalence about living. She had experienced disappointment and anger in her relationship to the women in the temple who did not come to rescue her. How much of her feelings were merging into my own consciousness? How could I integrate the Incan maiden into my being?

As I mentioned earlier, I attended a five-day workshop at the A.R.E. in Virginia Beach on past lives in July/August of 1980. It was called "Re-Awakening Constructive Patterns from Past Lives." The lecturers were Hugh Lynn Cayce, Dr. Charles Thomas Cayce (Edgar's son and grandson, respectively), Dr. Herbert and Meredith Puryear, Dr. Harold J. Reilly, and Dr. Gina Cerminara. About 100 people were in the audience. The workshop was geared toward helping us recall past-life memories and then extract constructive patterns that we could use in this life. I was very excited and felt fortunate to be there. I felt too shy, though, to ask for attention during the question-and-answer periods, but during the breaks I felt free to talk about my past-life vision and felt wonderfully supported and accepted. I also met with Everett Irion, a respected Cayce researcher and expert on dreams. I discussed the experience with him in private. He thought I was lucky to have this experience, even though I felt much pain and sadness about it and could not discuss it without crying. He encouraged me to do my own work on understanding its meaning, and he said I should not let others interpret it for me.

I also discussed it with a sharing group I met with daily during my stay. We met for breakfast and shared dreams. We meditated in a pyramid the A.R.E. used to have on its property. We tested our ESP (mine was slightly above average) and gave each other sand packs on the beach. (Cayce said that the crystalline properties in the sands in Virginia Beach have healing benefits.) On the last morning we had breakfast with Gina Cerminara. Her book *Many Mansions* had originally caught my attention and opened a new world to me.

While at the Beach, I thought about the positive pattern inherent in the life of the Incan maiden and concluded that my love for my friends and trust in my teachers were integral parts of that pattern. There was also my love for God as the Sun, for music, and for a simple life. I had been content with very little. The last night in Virginia Beach I had the following vivid dream:

I was with my mother in a professional building. We brought the bodies of eight or ten small children who had been dead for centuries into a room and put them on a large bed. They were wrapped in sheets, and I avoided touching their skin. They were so fragile that I was afraid they might come apart as I touched them, like very old mummies. I carefully carried one little dead body after another and laid it on the bed.

When they were all in the room and my mother had stepped out, one of the children opened her eyes. I was astonished. Then all the other children opened their eyes and started crawling about the room. I feared that they would crawl out of the room and into the hall where people might see them. I felt that the existence of these children was a secret.

I went to find my mother to ask for her help. I learned that a long time ago there had been a handsome, young, and rich man who had many girlfriends, who all got pregnant and had his babies. Somehow all the babies got killed.

The children who came back to life and whom we were taking care of were those love children.

To interpret this dream, I followed the five-step dream interpretation program in a now out-of-print A.R.E. dream course called "Awakening the Dreamer." For step five, "preliminary understanding," I wrote in my dream journal:

> "The little children are the good and healthy thoughts and feelings that were the result of a loving life lived and loving relationships I had with other girls and women among the Incas in Peru. The children being dead for many centuries means that my good thoughts and feelings about others died. The activities in Virginia Beach at the conference and relating the experience of Peru with my sharing group and with Everett Irion have brought me together with my Higher Self (the dream-mother), and at her initiative the thoughts and feelings are brought to life again. Such thoughts included: People care about me. People want me to live. People want my company. I don't have to die for anybody. I can live my life the way I want to. I am not helpless. No one is responsible for my life or my death."

Upon re-reading the chapter "The Lonely Ones" in *Many Mansions*, I came across a passage in which Gina Cerminara quoted Manly Hall from his book *Reincarnation: The Cycle of Necessity.* Manly Hall said that the usual karmic consequences of self-destruction, i.e., suicide, is that a future personality will die under conditions where the desire for life will be the greatest. Isn't that interesting, I thought. If I were the Incan maiden, and I had no doubt about it, then that had already happened to me. As the Incan maiden, I experienced a life of beauty and learned to value life. Ever since I recovered the memories of that life, my will to live had been strengthened.

Chapter 6
Mothering

Rejoice in the Great Play of the Mother of the World! The old world rejected the Mother of the World, but the New World begins to perceive Her lustrous veil.

—(From: *Mother of the World*, by Helena Roerich)

ONCE back in New York from the workshop in Virginia Beach, I had to put my interest in past lives on the back burner for a while and turn my attention to earning money. I had fully enjoyed one year of study at The New School for Social Research, had earned thirty-three credits during that time. After a few false starts, I became executive secretary to the executive vice president at the International Peace Academy (IPA). The IPA was founded by a wealthy woman from Philadelphia who reasoned that this country had academies that taught how to make war—West Point, for instance—so there should also be academies that taught how to make peace.

During the time I worked there, my boss, John Mroz, a

young man of Polish descent, made two trips to the Middle East, met with ministers and politicians, and wrote a book about security issues. I worked with him on the book and when it was released, we had a publication party across the street at the United Nations, inviting UN and Mission staff. I and two other secretaries were expected to go. "You have a very important job to do," said General Rikhye, the president of the IPA. "You have to take care of all the shy ambassadors." Sure enough, some ambassadors were truly shy and appreciated being asked if they would like more refreshments.

During these years I took several courses in dream study with a married couple who were members of the A.R.E., Joseph and Kathleen Meade. They lived in the Inwood area of Manhattan, and I took the famous "A" train to get there. Both were experts in dreams. They taught introductory, intermediate, and advanced dream courses. I took all three. Dreams were so fascinating. "Movies I watch when I'm asleep," a child once called them.

There were usually four or five people who gathered in the Meades' apartment. Kathleen would serve all kinds of herbal teas. Joseph systematically taught the meaning of the symbols that appeared in dreams. One particular day he discussed the symbolic meanings of the various body parts. Hair related to thinking, he said. Tangled hair could represent tangled thinking. Clean and orderly hair could represent clean and orderly thinking. He explained each part of the body in dreams, ending with the feet. He said the feet had to do with the principles of the dreamer and the foundation on which beliefs were built.

After the formal teaching, every student had the opportunity to share a dream and get help from both Joseph and Kathleen. Usually I brought in happy and pleasant dreams and avoided unpleasant ones as "not being important." But Joseph said something I never forgot about a frightening dream I shared once. He said, "Be thankful for your nightmares because they teach you what you really need to know." So, then I brought in the latest dream, whatever it was. Occasionally he would say about a dream, "That's a good one. You really hit pay dirt there." After he pointed out these things, I understood.

When I shared the dream of 10 May 1975, in which my mother told me that she had not cared about me at all, I expressed anger and resentment toward her. Joseph said bluntly, "The mother in your dreams represents your karma. She has kept your karma for you from your past lives and brings it to you again so that you can continue with your lessons where you left off." That hurt.

He further said that the Edgar Cayce readings teach that dreams must be examined on at least two levels, the literal and the symbolic. The dream mother might represent my biological mother but she might also represent the mother part in my own personality and be a symbol for my karmic fault of my own lack of love for me. The dream mother's willingness to comfort me seemed to be a promise of future love. I struggled to understand the symbol's dual meaning.

Carl Jung wrote that negative female characters in a woman's dream represent her shadow. The shadow contains all those qualities in yourself that you have rejected and disowned. That meant, according to Jung, that I had refused to accept the truth about my lack of self-love and was projecting it onto my mother. I could continue to deny that I did not love myself and blame my mother, or I could accept responsibility and learn to love me.

I now believe that while in relationships with others, we work through our feelings for ourselves by projecting them onto others. Others serve us as we serve them in this way. Another important relationship that we have is with ourselves, with the divine soul inside us. When this relationship is one of love, all our other relationships will be loving as well. But, rather than working in isolation on our inner relationship with God, we can use relationships with people, especially with our parents, to help clean up that inner relationship.

Ever since my father died, my mother would visit the family in New York every two or three years. I didn't have space to accommodate her, but would visit her wherever she was staying. My mother was somewhat like a child when she came to visit. She made no decisions about where to go, but followed the suggestions and wishes of whoever was her hostess at the time. At her visit in 1976, I wanted her to visit me in my new apartment in Manhattan. Peter and the group backed me up, agreeing that I should ask her.

Communication in my family was often limited to certain words and phrases. Much was taken for granted, and language was used to manipulate others and maintain power over them. I was breaking out of that pattern. After I had invited my mother to visit me, Kati, at whose house she was staying, called me on the phone one day, and I recorded our conversation in my journal. She said:

"I have tried to reach you for a long time. Have you been walking the streets?" She used a German word that Mother used on me and my sisters when we were teen-agers and stayed out longer than pleased her. It caused instant guilt and shame, but no one ever objected to it or talked about its exact meaning. "I am not a streetwalker," I protested.

"Oh, come on," she said. "I didn't mean that."

"But that is what you said," I replied. "You implied that I may have been walking the streets."

"I can tell you are in a bad mood," she snapped.

"No, I feel just fine," I said. Then, she dropped the subject and said, "Mother wants to speak with you."

My mother said, "Isn't it easier for you to come to visit me than for me to visit you?" What I heard between the lines was, "You are not important enough for me to visit you."

"I have a new apartment," I said, "and I would like you to see it. Is it really impossible for you to come to visit me?"

"Well, no," she said. "As a matter of fact, Tina and Bernhard have offered to drive me there."

"Well, there you are," I said.

"But I don't know if they are free the day you invited me to come. Tina is moving, you know," she said. But I heard, "You are not important. Tina is moving. She is important." Resisting the pressure to feel worthless and give in, I fought to stay connected to my desire for her visit.

"Can you ask them and find out?" I asked.

"Did you hear what I said?" Mother repeated irritably. "Tina is moving. She's moving." I felt more pressure to sacrifice my wishes, my equality, and my satisfaction.

"Yes," I said, "I heard you. Tina is moving. Will you call me back and let me know if you can come?"

"O.K.," she said meekly.

I was shaking when I got off the phone. The energy of both my fear and my strength coursed through my veins. I had held my ground and won the battle. Mother visited me on the day I had invited her.

That morning Heinz called at nine and said that he and Mother were at the German consulate in Manhattan. Was I home for them to come to visit me? I said, "Of course. I am expecting you." I opened the door when they rang the bell and shook their hands. Heinz's wife, Klara, was with them and so was Kati. I invited them in, pointed out the couches, and offered them coffee or tea.

"Do you have a bathroom?" Kati asked me. I was feeling good that they were in my apartment, and I felt strong to be myself, not timid, not afraid of their disapproval.

"No," I said, with a grin, "I don't have a bathroom. You've got to piss out the window." Everyone laughed.

Mother picked up her handbag and took out three paperback books.

"Here. I brought these for you."

They were books I had asked for. One was about the peculiar nature of the people in Niedersachsen, the county in which I grew up. Two books were in *Plattdeutsch*, the ancient German dialect I spoke as a child with my family, in which very few books are printed. I leaned against the round table by the window and held the books in my sensitive hands. Mother sat on the couch and I felt a new emotion toward her.

While the talk went on, I asked inside to find out what the feeling was and was surprised to get a clear sense that what I was feeling was love. I wanted to give my mother a kiss, but I didn't know how to kiss this woman who had never kissed me, who had touched me only to hurt me, who had used me as an object to receive her frustration and hatred. But she had brought me what I desired and that was an act of love. I felt grateful. She was not used to giving or taking physical affection, and I was afraid if I just bent over her she might feel I was attacking her. So I verbalized what I wanted to do:

"I want to give you a kiss for bringing me these books."

"No, no," she replied. "I don't want anything for the books."

"You don't understand. I want to give you a kiss."

"Oh, O.K.," she said and sat poised like a child, holding her face still for me to kiss her cheek.

Later, to hold them a little longer in my territory—Manhattan—I suggested an outing to the top of the World Trade Center. I rode with them in Heinz's car. It was cramped in the back seat and nonchalantly I put my arm through Mother's, deliberately breaking the rule of "no touching." She did not object, but seemed to like it.

Afterward we headed for the German restaurant *Hindenburg* on 86th Street and were seated at a table. Mother was on a roll of anger . . .

" . . . and the Nazis in Köhlen had it all planned. If Hitler won the war, the Kenners were to get our farm. We were going to be shipped to Russia, to the Ukraine . . . " Mother scolded as if it were our fault.

"Why?" I asked.

"Because Kenner was a Nazi and in the Party," she replied.

"Do you remember what Papa said about that?" Heinz asked.

"No, what did he say?"

"He said, 'They should have shipped us to the Ukraine. I would have gone right away. The best farmland in all of Europe is in the Ukraine.' "

I laughed so hard I screamed. My father had been an optimist, and this remark was typical of him. Mother dominated the talk as always and launched into another story, one about Grandma and Grandpa. After dinner, I said goodby with a handshake for everyone. But I hugged my mother.

I had a friend who, like me, struggled to recover from her mother's verbal abuse. She had decided to confront her mother and to treat her as she had been treated. She turned the tables and gave her mother the same ugly hostility she had received from her.

"If she can do it to me, I can do it to her," she reasoned.

My friend may have thought I was a coward because I chose not to confront my mother, but I had my reasons. I expected my mother would conveniently forget, deny, or minimize her hurtful behavior toward me, or put the blame on me for my sensitivity. I knew that taking revenge would not lead to the healing that I desired and might create negative karma. Besides, I knew I could work on my side of the relationship, heal my emotional pain, and change my attitudes without hurting her.

During this time I also became acquainted with a Jain teacher, Chitrabhanu or Gurudev (teacher), as most people called him. For a year or two I went every Thursday night to the Jain Meditation Center on East 86th Street to listen to Gurudev lecture. Jainism is an Indian religion in which harmlessness is an ultimate value. Jains observe strict rules to avoid killing any living creatures. Naturally they are vegetarians. Gurudev was a very gentle teacher. What attracted me most to him was that he frequently lectured about emotions. From Peter I learned the psychological point of view about emotions, but from Gurudev I learned the spiritual point of view.

I had followed a meditation practice for many years that called for using the mind to reach higher states of consciousness. So, I was amazed when Gurudev said, "Sometimes when you meditate you laugh, and sometimes you cry."

A student piped up and asked, "You want us to cry when we meditate?"

"No," said Gurudev, "I don't want you to cry. What I am saying is that when you meditate, you must let yourself be free to feel anything that comes up for you. You must not repress your feelings. If you feel like laughing, laugh; and if you feel like crying, cry. When you feel sad, you must feel it. Then you can ask God to take it from you and give you gladness instead."

Yoga and meditation classes were also held at the Center, and I attended many of them. His talks helped me to release negative feelings and replace them with positive ones. Once he addressed the pain faced by those who experienced difficulties in childhood. "Yes," he said, "childhood abuse is very painful. But the opportunities for advanced learning outweigh the pain. Nearly all the people I know who suffered in their early years have learned lessons they would not have learned had they had an easy childhood."

I spent two years in a therapy group with Peter as leader. Those two years opened the door to my inner life by only a crack, however, as Peter could not help me to open the door fully. At the time, neither I nor Peter apparently knew how deep the feelings were that I had repressed from the earliest years of my life. But I felt those feelings in my gut as a powerful force, like a volcano that wanted to erupt. Peter wanted an organized group with civilized clients who behaved properly and didn't muss their suits or dresses while they expressed themselves in neat sentences.

Once while working in group, I regressed to the consciousness of the little girl I used to be. I felt the injustice that had been done to me and my pain and rage. I wanted to get rid of those feelings, and for just a moment I behaved like a hurt and angry child about to throw a temper tantrum. But Peter was judgmental of my feelings and labeled my behavior as "wrong." He yelled at me to stop. I felt as if he had turned into my mother who had often yelled me into silence, even when I was still in the bassinet. I only attended group with Peter for a while longer, as I could not put my full trust in him any more. He had hurt me too much.

In retrospect, I am grateful to Peter for everything that he taught me and for the work we did together. The most important lesson I learned from him was about the three psychological positions on the "Rescue Triangle"—Rescuer, Persecutor, and Victim. Eric Berne, the founder of Transactional Analysis, first wrote about the "Rescue Triangle" in *Games People Play.* I identified most often as the "victim" and secondly as the "rescuer." Since then I have learned that my "victim" consciousness actually comes from past lives, when I was frequently literally a victim. From Peter I learned that when I identify myself as "victim," I have neither power nor love. "Mind is the builder," as Edgar Cayce often said, and what I think, I bring about. Subsequently I observed my thoughts, red-flagged all those that came from my "victim consciousness," neutralized, and then transformed them into the "hero," "warrior," and "victor" consciousness. In the book *Scripts People Live,* author Claude M. Steiner writes about how parents unwittingly train their children to be loveless, joyless, or powerless. He explains the decisions children make as a result of such training, and how, as adults, we can change these decisions and admit love, joy, and power back into our lives.

My mother's 1976 visit had unblocked more memories of her verbal violence and my pain. Often I seemed to be enveloped and filled with darkness when I wanted to be surrounded and filled by light. I learned, however, that healing is not a straight journey into the light, but that we have to look at the negativity, the ugliness of the pain and what caused it, and get to know both intimately before we can heal it. It is a dirty job. I cooperated with the natural process and worked with what came into consciousness, but I often doubted the necessity of looking at the pain and the ugly causes of that pain. My childhood had been one long training session in denying pain and unhappiness and faking happiness. My resistance was powerful, and I needed encouragement to go on.

A psychic healer and workshop leader gave me a statement from the apocryphal *Gnostic Gospel of Thomas* that was like a magic key for some time: "If you bring forth what is within you, what you bring forth will save you. If you do not bring forth what is within you, what you do not bring forth will destroy you."

Another encouragement came from the myth of the twelve labors of Hercules, the universal disciple who has to make conscious the contents of his subconscious mind, the monstrous hydra from the deep. He had to kneel and humbly lift them into the light of day. There they lost their power and died. So I, too, had to become conscious of my monsters, fears, feelings of worthlessness, shame, and guilt.

It was an odd experience to consciously fill my mind one moment with monsters, with my ugly and horrible memories, my feelings of pain, shame, and guilt, then willfully turn them over to God, and then fill my mind with lofty and pure spiritual principles. All that this practice required to be effective was courage and humility. I found that by lifting negative feelings or a negative experience into consciousness and telling God about it, the negativity around it evaporated. When I next became aware of the same old pain of a memory, it had changed. There was less negativity, less pain, and more understanding and compassion.

I was conscious of my fear of violence and my dreams made me aware of my potential for violence and of my hidden rage. In one dream my mother's body was chopped into large chunks and went round and round in a washing machine. In another, it was chopped up and hidden in a huge chest, where I discovered it. I was a research scientist in the dream and took notes on the body. Another figure of my mother, living and breathing, stood by and curiously watched me.

A female therapist, whom I saw only once, was, however, right on target when she said about my mother: "She really said those things to you? Maybe some women think them, but they wouldn't say them out loud to their child. It sounds as if she was psychotic for a time." Sick people, I thought, need healing, not condemnation.

While searching for someone else with whom to continue my own healing process, I read voraciously. Books by Krishnamurti, *Think on These Things* and *Commentaries on Living*, influenced my thinking. He encouraged me to observe my thought processes. He said, and I paraphrase, "Don't follow the old beaten track of traditional thinking. Think afresh for yourself." Existentialist writers, such as Camus, Sartre, and Unamuno attracted my attention. Carl Jung's autobiography, *Memories, Dreams, Reflections*, was my favorite during that time because it combined psychological insight with transcendental and subjective personal experiences.

In January 1978, I watched the NBC evening news and saw a five-minute clip on a new therapy developed by Dr. Daniel Casriel. It was called the New Identity Process. The clip showed a woman standing on the floor and screaming out childhood pain from deep in her belly while someone warmly held her in his arms. Tears streamed down her cheeks. She took a deep breath, then screamed again. As her pain subsided, her screams changed. Then stopped. She opened her eyes. The camera was right on her face. She looked relaxed and then smiled with obvious relief and pleasure. I was entranced. Here was what I needed. But could I, a shy country girl from another country, overcome my inhibitions and scream publicly in a group of tough native New Yorkers? To find out I made an appointment at the Casriel Institute, saw a longer videotaped session, was interviewed by Frankie Wiggins, a therapist, and admitted into her weekly group.

I learned that the founder of the New Identity Process, Dr. Casriel, had worked with drug-addicted patients at Daytop Village, New York, in the sixties and pioneered the healing work of using direct emotional expression. First, he worked with patients to release their negative emotions: fear, pain, and anger. Second, he taught them to experience and create the feelings of pleasure and love. His book, *A Scream Away from Happiness*, describes his group therapy practice, during which he would suggest an appropriate statement, called a "tool," to the client to verbalize in order to bring up the repressed emotion. When the negative emotion had been released, and the client was conscious of the negative thought that had caused it, he would suggest a positive thought to be worked with and accepted for the future.

Within a week I found myself sitting in a circle of seventeen adults in a large mirrored room on the second floor of the Institute. Nearly everyone in the circle was relaxed and at ease. Like children, they unashamedly held hands with the person to the right and left. I was surprised to see mattresses placed inside and outside the circle.

Frankie, the leader of this group, began the meeting by holding a "go-around." She asked each person in turn, "How was your week?" When someone shared an experience that kicked up feelings of fear, pain, or anger which were clearly visible in the person's face, she said, "Hold that feeling for the 'group scream' and work with it later, too." As a newcomer, I sat next to Frankie. I listened to everyone's report of events and feelings that had been experienced during the week. The honesty of these people about their experiences and their feelings was extraordinary and fascinated me.

The fourth person to share that night, a young man from Switzerland, struggled with obvious feelings of deep grief and could barely continue to talk. "All right," Frankie said, "stop talking, scream out the feeling!" He grabbed tighter the hands of the persons on the right and left, filled his whole body with a deep breath, opened his mouth—and let a scream emerge. The other people in the room remained calm and watched him with interest, sharing in his pain with compassion.

I had never been in the same room with a human being who screamed with all his power, like this young man. I was reminded of animals in pain and in fear of death. The screams were bloodcurdling. I was scared. But another part of me was fascinated. Something unusual was happening here. My fear won over the fascination. Strong feelings kicked up in my belly. I felt as if my feelings were going to overflow, no, burst out, with an energy that was beyond horror and terror, a boundless, nameless mass of powerful raw emotional energy. Frankie turned to me and asked: "What do you think?" I said, "I think people are being born here tonight." Then she asked gently: "And what do you feel?" I said one word, "Scared." She said, "Can you scream it out?" I replied, "I think so."

She then knelt in front of me and held her arms tightly around my waist to reassure me. Tears sprang to my eyes immediately. I felt the pressure of years of repressed childhood fear and pain welling up in my guts and Frankie's warm arms around me. I took a deep breath and screamed. She held me like a mother, like the mother I had always wanted, warm and reassuring. She was there for me and only for me. I could feel the warm life in her arms, her body, and her face. I had never felt my mother's body in that comforting way. The fear and terror just tumbled out of my throat with a sound such as I had never made before in my life. I was scared, but oh, it was so good to let it go. I screamed as I had seen the young man scream, taking deep breaths in between. I stopped screaming when the pressure inside me abated. I was exhausted. "Good work," said Frankie, and she gave me a big smile.

During my turn in the "go around" I told a little bit of my story, then listened to others, watched them work, and worked more myself. Toward the end of the meeting, Frankie said to a handsome young man with a southern accent, "George, Jennifer has worked enough for today. Take her down on the mat; you know what to do." He explained to me that after you have expressed fear, pain, or anger, you are entitled to take in pleasure and love. He was going to lie down with me on a mat, amongst all the people, and simply hold me in his arms. We lay down, and he held me like an older brother, like a big warm teddy bear. He talked to that part in me that was childlike and complimented me sincerely for the work he had watched me do and told me how much I deserved to receive pleasure and love because, he said, "You are *lovable*."

I walked home through Manhattan after that first session, and I knew that in Frankie I had found the right therapist and my next teacher. Before she became a therapist, she had actually been a teacher. I felt certain that she could take me through areas of deep emotions in my psyche into which Peter had been afraid to venture.

After several months of group work, I consulted Frankie in a private session about working in the group on my past-life trauma. Would the group think I was crazy, ridicule me, and not want to hold my hand any more? Frankie didn't think so and encouraged me to take the risk. So, during the next group session I explained my memory of a brief life in Peru, being chosen as a sacrifice, and the painful emotions that I was repressing. "When I'm with people," I concluded, "I still feel that I should sacrifice me, my feelings, my opinions, my very self, for their benefit."

I sensed that some members in the group had a fascination about past-life memories to which they were not quite willing to admit. But mostly they felt that it doesn't matter if past lives are true, but that what I was feeling was true, and that was all that mattered. Frankie suggested that I lie on my back on one of the mats in the center and the others gather around. She asked me to close my eyes and go back in time. I did that and opened my mind to the memories. Within a moment, I was filled with the sum total of my experience in that lifetime. With a conscious effort to also be aware of my surroundings in the room, I listened to Frankie's suggestion that I use as the first tool the statement "I want to live." I screamed it, first gently then louder. Tears flowed, my nose ran. My body seemed to drown in the pain of having been sacrificed and was on fire with the desire to live.

With each scream more of the ancient pain was released, and after several minutes of screaming, I lay on the mat breathing deeply and at peace. Frankie said, "O.K., that was good. Now say: 'I don't have to sacrifice me any more.'" I nodded and took a deep breath and began by gently saying it. Pain kicked up immediately. As a child, I had habitually sacrificed my needs, feelings, and opinions for my brothers and sisters as well as my parents. And I was still doing it in this very group. The pain was followed by screams of anger toward people who not only accepted but expected my self-sacrifice. Anger gave way to strength and the conviction that I don't have to do it any more. Warm and gentle hands stroked me and told me how welcomed I was.

When I walked out into the street after this particular session, I felt lighter than ever before. An ancient grief and sadness that had weighed me down from before I was born was no longer there. On a very deep level, beyond the mental and emotional, my awareness of myself had changed. Now I could stand back from the experience, get it into proper perspective, and integrate the life as an Incan maiden into my present life as immigrant, secretary, and student of metaphysics in New York City.

I could accept the Incan maiden's devotion to the Sun God, her purity, her creativity, flute playing, and weaving, and add them to my own creativity. I could replace my reality of feeling unworthy by breathing in her reality of being loved and honored by her people. I could replace my reality of feeling unwanted and unloved by breathing in her reality of being wanted and loved.

I reflected wryly on having something few other people had: a crystal-clear memory of a past life. But far from the idealized image many people have of their past lives, thinking of themselves as having been Cleopatra or the Queen of Sheba, I had been an insignificant Native American maiden who had been forced to give up her life as a human sacrifice. Not much to brag about, but an important piece of information for me in understanding my life.

Frankie was very much loved by her clients, old and young. One of the most important lessons I learned in her group was that it is far more painful to repress pain and to hold onto it in secret, than to admit that it is there, to feel it, and to release it. For months I worked on releasing my fear of my mother and the grief she had caused me. I reached that part of my psyche where, if I as much as remembered and formed a mental picture of my mother, I would feel fear and pain and instantly could release it by screaming. Frankie gave me many "tools" to work with to facilitate the release, such as, "You don't control me any more," "I don't have to please you any more," and "I'm good enough."

Even though the New Identity Process was not a spiritual process as such, spirituality was there. Frankie, for instance, was one of the most loving human beings I have ever met. She was fair in giving her attention to group members, neither neglecting nor preferring anyone. She told us that the New Identity Process could sometimes get us into a place of fear and despair when we were not in group. She gave us her home telephone number and said, "If you really need me, call me, even if it is three o'clock in the morning."

I added a measure of spirituality on my own when I worked. I used the "tools" Frankie had given me and soon learned which worked best for me. When I finished working with one "tool" and my screams subsided, I silently asked my Higher Self, the divine part that was aware on a level that I was not, which "tool" to use next. Then I listened. Invariably I received a "tool" that was workable from the still, small voice inside. I worked on releasing fear and pain, but I could seldom reach my anger.

I learned that working only in English did not touch certain parts of my subconscious mind, and so I had to translate into German and especially *Plattdeutsch* those beliefs I wanted to incorporate into my belief system. The great psychoanalysts, Freud and Jung, confirmed that we must translate our new beliefs into the language of our childhood, because that is what the subconscious mind still speaks.

My dreams became clearer and more vivid during this time and were often like stories; with a beginning, a middle, and an end. Interesting new symbols appeared, powerful bears and wolves, a village idiot with three eyes, a beautiful woman who lived in a castle, and a mysterious woman from another life and another planet. I acquired a stronger feeling of my own identity as a person with my own boundaries. I used the mind to build, literally, a new personality. This mental work could not have been done by my human ego or personality, but I believe it was done under the guidance of my divine soul.

I constantly invoked God's help. When it came, it was often uncanny and miraculous. In the beginning of this mental healing work, I searched my mind every morning after meditation, usually while walking to the office, for negative beliefs that might still be operating. The second step was to release them and listen for a positive statement from my higher self. Then I used that positive statement as an affirmation for the rest of that day. The statements that came to me could be anything from psychological ones, such as "I am good enough," to spiritual ones, such as "Be still and listen" or "I am a divine child of God."

During these months I also became more creative. I began to sing again, using spiritual poetry and prayers as lyrics, making up the melodies as I went along. I let my child ego state speak to my newly created parent ego state, the inner loving mother, as well as to the divine mother goddess force in the universe. "Hold me, love me, care about me. Kiss me, softly, I need your love, to heal my hurt, I need to see your face, loving me." Occasionally I was able to visualize my mother's face smiling at me, loving me, and then I felt as if I had connected to her Higher Self, which had always loved me.

Chapter 7
Possibilities

> Occasionally when hiking in canyons or mountainous regions I have been attuned to the exuberant calls the Mountain Devas shout to each other across chasms or ridges.
>
> —(*Natives of Eternity*, by Flower A. Newhouse)

JOSEPH and Kathleen Meade gave another dream course in 1979 and I attended it. I had begun to read other authors on dreams: Ann Faraday, Kathleen Jenks, Tony Crisp. I was close to several people in the New York A.R.E. community: Ruth Fortrel, who taught numerology and sketching; Alan Steele and Robert Hendrickson, who helped Study Groups get started. Robert also worked on the New York A.R.E. newsletter, *The Open Door*, and I helped type articles and announcements of future events. Before the age of word processors, every page had to be typed so that it could be photocopied. I wrote a few small pieces myself, a review of William James's *Varieties of Religious Experience*, which Edgar Cayce had recommended that everyone ought to read, a short piece about the wonderful physical sensations of loving someone, and a somewhat larger piece (a whole page) on the A.R.E. dream groups in New York.

Christmas 1979, my friend and former roommate, Erika, came to visit me. I had not seen her since 1968 when she had suddenly decided to return to Germany and to study nursing in Hamburg. After she had left New York, she wrote to me and asked if I had not found it strange that during the two years she lived with me that she had never dated anyone. I had not found it strange as her English had been poor, and she had been busy with her creative pursuits.

She wrote that when she returned to Germany, it had become clear to her that men did not interest her. She had found a woman to love. They had moved into the same apartment and expected to spend the rest of their lives together. At first, I tried to reason with her in my letters and talk her out of it. But then I realized that I did not know the purpose of her soul, and I could not judge her nor could I dictate to her how she should live her life. Perhaps she had been a man in many lifetimes and had loved women and was not ready in this life to switch to loving men. I felt, however, that I had a strong positive connection with her, probably from past lives in which we had known each other. Our connection had also survived two years of being roommates and ten years of sharing our different life styles in our letters.

She told me in her correspondence that she had become a feminist and had gone on many demonstrations for women. She sent me an article published in a German women's magazine about her "coming out" and publicly proclaiming that she was a lesbian. When she "came out" in the hospital where she was working as a psychiatric nurse, she kept me informed of her feelings about her colleagues as they responded, either with fear and withdrawal or with love and understanding.

I must admit that I had some trepidation about having her as my guest for two weeks. When she arrived, I was presented with a fully self-loving woman. Where I still struggled to undo the years of habitually repressing my feelings, Erika indulged and glorified hers. While I was struggling to overcome my learned attitude that love and tender feelings for anyone else are a weakness, her self-love and her concern for and need of others was open and without shame. She took elaborate pleasure in eating (she was slim), in feeling sunshine on her skin, and in watching men and women walk. She was never in a hurry, but gave herself all the time she needed to be comfortable and at ease.

She never reproached herself, never seemed to feel guilty, but always was gentle and understanding with herself. In her walks around the city, alone or with me, she was fearless. She took photographs of unusual sights that struck her fancy—fire hydrants, tall buildings, and especially people who looked unusual or unconventional. She never hesitated to snap photos, even of unpredictable street people, and she communicated adequately with just a few words of English.

While she was with me, she showered me with tender, loving motherly and sisterly attention that no other woman, save Frankie, had ever given me. She made my apartment a warm place by being in it. She truly accepted herself and other women. Why couldn't men love women with the same kind of acceptance? Why couldn't I love myself that way? Or could I?

For two weeks Erika and I talked and argued. We went to feminist book stores, and she helped me pick out books to read. With one fell swoop she broke down my defenses about the feminist movement. Throughout the two weeks, arguments and all, I was fascinated by this woman who fearlessly made her own way in the world. "I have to be happy with me," she said. "I have to be true to myself. And I am. People either accept me the way I am, or they don't." In retrospect, I can see how self-indulgent she was. But I was still at the opposite end of the spectrum—still self-sacrificing and self-effacing. Neither position was ideal. As it was, however, I learned from her how I might adjust my position.

She had come at just the right moment when I was ready to be imprinted with a new image of my womanhood and when I was ready to begin a long and slow inquiry into myself as a female member of human society. Her visit created a desire to find out more about myself as a woman on this planet and about giving and taking love as a woman in relationships with other people.

After she left, I joined a political women's consciousness-raising group through the National Organization for Women (N.O.W.). This group met weekly for eight months, and we discussed many aspects of our lives as women living in a patriarchal society. I did not care very much at the time for the political aspect of the sponsoring organization, a little spirituality injected into it would have gone a long way, but I came to care for all the women in the group the more I learned about their lives, their suffering, and their hopes.

I felt frustrated that my salary at the nonprofit Peace Academy did not enable me to continue college. After two years, I looked around and found a job that would pay enough and also promised to give me the opportunity to write. I interviewed my future employer as well as was interviewed by him. We met with each other three times. I thought I had a winner. But the first day on the job told me it was a lemon. Suddenly, my employer was no longer the cultured and creative gentleman he had purported to be, but an impatient and critical taskmaster and, worst of all, a rage-oholic.

After the first day on the job, I dreamed of horses crashing on a bobsled course, mortally wounded or dead, and I woke up in a cold sweat. I knew something was going to crash and die in my life, and I suspected it would be the job. In New York State, if you quit a job, you cannot collect unemployment insurance. Since I had little savings, I hoped that he would fire me. Thankfully, after two weeks I was free, but I felt as if the rug had been pulled out from under my feet. I had had the best intentions in wanting to work hard, earn good money, get a college education, and fit myself for higher work. Was this my karma? Had I fired *him* during some past life? Perhaps. If it was karmic, I could not do better than take to heart these words of the fourteen-year-old Krishnamurti in a little booklet called *At the Feet of the Master*: "You must bear your karma cheerfully, whatever it may be, taking it as an honor that suffering comes to you, because it shows that the Lords of Karma think you worth helping. However hard it is, be thankful that it is no worse."

I visited the unemployment office, and on my next monthly meditation report to the Arcane School mentioned that I was without a job. I promptly received a note from Mary Bailey, the second wife of Foster Bailey and now the president of Lucis Trust, of which the Arcane School is a part, inviting me to phone her and set up an interview as she needed a secretary. I could hardly believe the letter in my hands. But I remembered that already six years earlier, in 1975, when I still worked at the *Daily News*, she had offered me this position. At that time I had turned it down because it involved massive stenography which, although I had always managed to take down and transcribe the dictation I was given, I had no love for it. But another reason I had turned it down was that I did not feel worthy to be a part of such a wonderful spiritual organization that served so many people all over the planet.

Now, it seemed, God left me no choice. It seemed He wanted me at Lucis Trust. Now, however, I also saw the tremendous opportunity for my personal growth and growth in my ability to be of service to the world. I still did not feel worthy, but now I was willing to confront these feelings. The interview with Mary, as she asked me to call her, went well. I agreed to begin working with her the following Monday. Walking home and remembering our discussion about salary, I thought that God was playing a cosmic joke on me. I would be paid according to my need to meet expenses for rent, food, and clothing. Nothing for entertainment. Nothing for college. Would I ever finish my education? Or would I be a "drop-out" for the rest of my life?

No longer relying on giving dictation, Mary had switched a few years before to using a dictaphone machine. The major part of my work consisted of transcribing her correspondence. It seemed each letter contained something fascinating and helpful to my understanding. I also retyped articles for the magazine *The Beacon*, typed Mary's speeches, and entered four sixty-page study sets onto the new word processor that nobody else wanted to touch. There was no one to teach me its use. By trial and error I learned setting margins, adjusting page lengths, coding page numbers, etc. I enjoyed working with it very much and often stayed till late at night to master certain functions.

We numbered about twelve employees altogether, ten of whom were Arcane School students. The first thing we did at 9:15 in the morning was to silently take our places in the meditation room. This room was lit by a dim light that shone onto a painting of a blue five-pointed star and yellow triangle, set into an orange circle on a dark blue background. We then meditated with our eyes closed. We practiced several different kinds, none of which, however, were for personal benefit. We meditated for the purpose of bringing God's divine light and wisdom to humanity. The meditations required focusing on thoughts and images, and we used our wills to bring about these desired ends. The morning meditation period lasted five minutes or so.

At 12:00 noon we would enter the room again for a longer meditation of fifteen to twenty minutes, and once more at 5:00 p.m. for a brief linking up with the New Group of World Servers (a nonorganized group of people who had in common the giving of unselfish service) around the world. Each meditation ended with the Great Invocation, which had been dictated to Alice Bailey by the Tibetan lama:

The Great Invocation

From the point of Light within the Mind of God
Let light stream forth into the minds of men.
Let Light descend on Earth.

From the point of Love within the Heart of God
Let love stream forth into the hearts of men.
May Christ return to Earth.

From the center where the Will of God is known
Let purpose guide the little wills of men—
The purpose which the Masters know and serve.

From the center which we call the race of men
Let the Plan of Love and Light work out.
And may it seal the door where evil dwells.

Let Light and Love and Power restore the Plan on Earth.

In spite of my attempt to be true to myself and not repress my feelings, at the office I felt tempted to do just that. The high spiritual atmosphere at Lucis seemed to bear down on me and brought up unfinished emotional business. The vibrations literally forced out my negative energies. Old problems that I thought I had finished with came up again for review, albeit on a higher curve of the spiral. I was motivated to serve the highest and to sacrifice the lowest, but I tended to respond to authority with distrust, fear, and resistance. The other problem that came up for me was a strong feeling of shame. I had not realized how much shame I still repressed within my unconscious. So, I consciously decided to let the high spiritual vibration in the office do its work on me. I surrendered to the cleansing effect.

Several times I quickly left the office for short periods of time because of a sudden feeling of intense shame. I would close the door behind me and sit in a private place in the ladies room. I would close my eyes and consciously accept the shame. I studied shame and learned that it feels hot, confusing, embarrassing, painful, crazy, dirty, scary, and even demonic and poisonous. I learned that many of my emotions and behaviors were wrapped up in shame, which had made emotional expression so difficult for me. I realized that if I could accept and release my shame, I would have easier access to all of my emotions. After asking the divinity within to be with me and to guide me in my healing work, I would talk to my inner child of the past and assure her of my love. Together we would feel the shame. "It's O.K.," I would say. "You can feel it. It won't kill you. Feel it and let it go. I'll help you."

Also, in these situations I often talked to God directly, "God, I don't want this shame any more. Please take it away from me. Give me feelings of worthiness instead." If not the first approach, then the second would spark something in my psychic energies, and I would be able to cry. Just those few tears would open the way for the painful shame to be released. Touching up my make-up afterward and facing myself in the mirror, I would see a trace of sadness around my eyes and a new joy radiating from deep within me, enveloping me like a mantle, and making my steps light and easy. When I returned to the office, I would feel like a new person, fresh, clean, energized, and ready to smile again.

I was beginning to grow, but I still didn't feel as though all the pieces to my being were yet in place. I had no idea where I would gain the understanding I'd been seeking for so long. Because of my correspondence with Erika and my contacts with the National Organization for Women I became aware of the many societal pressures women received in various environments. N.O.W. had the intention to benefit women and used the legal and political arenas and wanted all women to be political. Erika took an interpersonal approach and focused on everyday loving relationships. I had grown up in a home and a national environment that was trapped in authoritarian, anti-feminine attitudes that assigned women to "Kinder, Kirche, and Küche" (children, church, and kitchen).

On a Saturday in 1981, I was listening to a radio program on WBAI and heard that a two-day spiritual workshop for women was taking place that weekend in a private apartment in Manhattan. This was the first time I ever considered women's spirituality as possibly being different from men's spirituality, and I was intrigued. At the workshop the next day, even though I knew no one there, I felt that I belonged.

At the end of the workshop everyone was still excited and did not want to go home. The woman who had organized and conducted this meeting, Gabrielle Beard, offered her studio apartment at Westbeth, the apartment building mostly occupied by artists, for future meetings. We decided to give our group a name and chose "Women and Wisdom." We had several workshops at Gabrielle's apartment and then rented a larger space, comprising several rooms, at Westbeth.

With about a dozen other women, I spent a weekend painting walls and ceilings of our new space and sewing dozens of throw pillows to lean against while sitting on the carpeted floors. As I was one of the founding members of

Women and Wisdom, I enjoyed preparing our new space for future meetings. Gabrielle arranged for Gloria Karpinski, a healer from Winston-Salem, North Carolina, and author of *Where Two Worlds Touch*, to come to Women and Wisdom and give workshops in healing, forgiveness, and manifesting abundance. Gloria did her name full justice—she was beautiful. She dressed in pastel-colored skirts and blouses of soft, flowing materials. She was a woman who had liberated herself from predominantly feminine stereotypes and was gentle and self-loving.

She told us about her experiences with healing. She was able to see a client's illness with her inner eye, in spiritual rather than medical terms, and worked with spirit guides on the inner plane to heal the conditions. She handled her gift with love and respect, giving credit to God or Spirit for any healing she was able to do.

During one particular workshop we experimented with psychometry. About thirty women sat in a large circle on the floor, leaning against the walls, softened by pillows. Each gave Gloria a personal object in a sealed envelope in an exercise to demonstrate invisible forces and abilities which, Gloria said, we all had but often did not acknowledge. She shuffled the envelopes and handed one to each woman. On cue, every woman opened her envelope, put the item in the left palm, and tried to receive impressions about the owner.

My envelope contained a gold bracelet. The instant I placed it in my left palm, a full-color image of Carmen's face, a woman present in the room, exploded between my eyebrows just inside my head in the place that is called the "third eye." What did that mean? My rational mind immediately became defensive and denied the significance.

I could accept out-of-body experiences and visions of a past life. These took place in the privacy of my own home. No one knew about them unless I told someone. But to experience third-eye activity in *public*, that was a different story. That was scary. I didn't know at the time, but would learn later, that in at least one past life in a small town in New England, I was murdered by a mob in public for having unusual psychic abilities. In those times psychic gifts were thought to be of the devil. Women who exhibited them were considered witches. It was no wonder then that I was scared when my third eye opened up in public.

We then did a round robin, and everyone shared the impressions she had received. Many women picked up facts about the owner's life. I shared my experience and was as thrilled as I was shocked to find that the bracelet I'd held actually belonged to Carmen. I marveled at each woman's perceptions, but I felt uneasy about my own.

Gloria said that we could use our hands to *see* in a way that would complement the power of our eyes. She said we could develop our skills by practicing them and encouraged us to experiment. During the following week I stood next to a rack of slacks and looked for the right size to take to the fitting room. As I handled one pair after another, I was more aware of my hands than usual. Looking at one particular pair and deciding they were the wrong size, I noticed that my hands, however, told me otherwise. They felt very comfortable with this pair, as if the slacks already had my vibration. If my hands could have spoken, they would have said, "These fit perfectly." I tried them on, found out that my hands were right, and bought them.

My hands have now become a more reliable guide to buying books than my mind. Somehow, my hands can feel the content of a book and know whether it is meaningful for me or not. My hands work together with my solar plexus chakra, one of the major energy centers in the body. If my solar plexus relaxes as a result of my hands holding a book, as if I am sighing and saying, "Ah yes, this is nice," then I am sure the book is right for me.

During breaks at the workshops at Women and Wisdom,

women often talked about "readings" they had with Gloria. They raved about how much she had helped them to better understand themselves and their lives. I often regretted that I had not been around to ask for a reading by Edgar Cayce. Although Cayce and Gloria gave different kinds of psychic readings, I now had a chance to get one by her, and so I put my name on the list.

Alone in my apartment the night before the reading, I prepared myself. Gloria had said to come with three or four questions, and I wrote mine down on paper. I knew that my state of mind at the time of the reading could influence its quality. The same is true for meditation, for which I prepared by being clean in body and mind. I used prayer and read sources of spiritual wisdom. I then browsed through *A Treatise on Cosmic Fire*, by Alice A. Bailey, a complicated book on cosmology, philosophy, and psychology. As I browsed, I came to a passage that contained a preposterous idea about "nature devas," divine spirits associated with the angel kingdom, which help govern the animal, vegetable, and mineral life forms, and who occasionally incarnated into the human kingdom. I thought this to be a far-fetched idea.

On the morning of my reading, September 20, 1981, I traveled to the west side of Manhattan and met Gloria in the upstairs room in a beautiful home of a friend of hers. I felt anxious about what I would find out. Gloria was calm and exuded peace. She made small talk for a minute, tested the tape recorder, and then she leaned back, offered a prayer for both of us, and my reading began. Unlike Cayce, Gloria remained conscious, with her eyes closed, throughout the reading.

"Let me begin," she said, "by saying that nobody knows what you are doing on this planet but you . . . At most, what I can do is to mirror for you from another perspective, give you some input to think about and to weigh, but nobody but you can know if that reflection is accurate or not . . . "

She sat opposite me on the easy chair, legs drawn up under her, leaning back, smiling with closed eyes, talking. I felt a slight anxiety and strangely elevated. I sensed that this beautiful woman opposite me was connected to a reality to which I had only limited access. I sensed a high energy or even a presence in the room that inspired me with awe. Without prompting, she addressed the unspoken question of my identity:

" . . . The way it's shown to me," she said, "is that you're like the bud of a plant that is rare, and you don't say, let's see what's in the center of this bud by pulling away the leaves. You just have to wait until it's ready to show itself, because it's unusual and because it's growing in an environment that is not its own. Underline that in red, please. This world is not your own; this is not your natural place, and so you feel at times like an alien. You have often felt in your life: what am I doing here, I don't belong here, this is a weird place."

She said that at this time in my life I was, metaphorically speaking, putting down my "root system" into planet Earth. I wanted to make myself very secure and depend on myself for this feeling of security, this feeling of groundedness. With such a foundation, I would no longer feel as vulnerable as I had, but be able to be myself and grow and unfold.

She continued to say that one of the biggest issues that I had to deal with in this life was how to express myself here and not to get crucified. She said I wanted and needed to learn how to exist in the density of the earth plane, where it was violent and hostile and where there were so many dense and negative thought forms—a situation to which I was unaccustomed, given this loftier realm which I supposedly called home. But, she said, what I was learning was that what I had to give was what the Taoists spoke of when they said that there was nothing softer in this world than water and nothing stronger.

She said that I would not have been open to this information when I was twenty-one, scared to death, and had had deep subconscious memories of having died violently, many times, on this planet. She said that there had been many times when I stayed out of incarnation for long periods because I was afraid. She said that on some level I found this planet a very crude place to be.

"Maybe," she said, "to really understand, we have to back up and ask who you are and where you are. What is shown to me is that the kingdom that you come from . . . You know, Jesus spoke of 'many mansions.' I interpret that to mean many realities. The place that is shown to me is a place of such radiance that it is beyond description."

She said it was a dimension that was not dangerous. Sensitivity was another chief characteristic of this dimension. "It is part of the kingdom of the angels. O.K., now I've said it. Do you know anything about the deva kingdom?" "Yes," I said, "a little."

"O.K., then," she continued, "I would say that I perceive you as originating from that stream of evolution. Now, this doesn't mean that you're not human, do you understand? A lot of devas take incarnation."

I sat on my chair and listened, entranced. The feeling was similar to the way I felt during a meditation when I succeeded in raising my consciousness to a higher level and sensed light from above flowing into my awareness. I felt as if suddenly a door had opened in my mind and a bright light flowed in. I was overjoyed and flooded with love. I felt as if I had had amnesia about my identity and now that it was over, my identity had been restored to me. It was just like in grammar school when I heard about the Native Americans for the first time and my mind said, "I always knew they were there. I'd just forgotten." Now my mind said, "I always knew I came from there. I'd just forgotten."

Gloria spoke for an hour and a half. At the end, she said a

prayer of gratitude and released all energies that were neither hers nor mine and opened her eyes. I hugged her good-by. I was overstimulated with all the new ideas. Many of them had existed in embryonic form within me, but came to life now because of the reading. The entire session was tape recorded, so I did not have to strain to remember any of it. I listened to the tape many times and eventually transcribed it.

What had Gloria told me? That my soul originated in the deva kingdom? Alice Bailey wrote that divine, God-created souls began incarnating in human bodies 18 to 21 million years ago and slowly evolved through repeated incarnations. Madame Blavatsky and clairvoyants such as Rudolf Steiner, Annie Besant, and Edgar Cayce stated that humanity had developed the physical body in ancient Lemuria, the emotional body on Atlantis, and was now developing mental faculties. In the future, we would develop pure intuition and telepathy.

Since first discovering reincarnation, I assumed I had incarnated on this planet for many millions of years. But when I psychically compared my inner and outer self with people around me, something did not add up. My inner self seemed to be ahead in its development, while my outer self was behind socially and emotionally. Sometimes I thought that a part of me was somehow defective. At other times I thought perhaps I had committed some horrible crime in a past life so that now God limited me so I would not get myself any deeper into trouble. I could not explain my acute emotional and intuitive sensitivity. Was it a weakness, or was it a blessing?

If I originated in the deva kingdom, that could explain why I felt often inwardly so different from my eight brothers and sisters. They were practical and down to earth. They had common sense, were occupied with earning a living in independent businesses and with making themselves physically comfortable. I wanted a formal education and did not care for money or comfort. I preferred to work for nonprofit organizations and volunteered my services for good causes and worked after hours without pay. They talked about the high cost of living, I talked about transforming negative emotions into positive ones and living with joy. They were at home in their physical bodies in this physical world. I was ethereal, elfin-like, a spirit of nature, who often found the physical world an "enormously crude place," as Gloria had indicated.

While the Edgar Cayce readings neither confirm nor deny it, Alice Bailey, an expert on esoteric wisdom, wrote that devas incarnate into the human kingdom. Had I not accidentally or synchronistically come across this passage, I might have dismissed Gloria's reading as fantasy. I found Alice Bailey's ideas as sound as Edgar Cayce's, and I could not dismiss this information. Of course, to avoid ridicule, I also could not tell my next-door neighbor, nor my brothers and sisters that I believed I descended from the angels. I had to keep it to myself and share it only with friends whom I trusted to treat the revelation with discretion.

How could I reconcile this information with that which came through Edgar Cayce? Cayce talked about angels, especially archangels and guardian angels. As a child, he saw nature spirits and played with them in his parents' back yard. He did not mention that angels could incarnate into the human kingdom. But did that mean it was impossible? I think not. Edgar Cayce gave health readings for twenty years before he even mentioned reincarnation. At first he was not at all comfortable with the information that had come through him.

Based on my personal research in esoteric literature, I have come to believe that devas choose to incarnate into the human kingdom in order to help human evolution and to continue their own evolution. The human kingdom is a gigantic classroom, and souls who incarnate into human bodies do so in order to learn to love and eventually to return to God.

The synchronicity of having read about devas the night before the reading, along with the reading itself, opened my eyes to this strange new possibility. I couldn't prove that I was an incarnate deva or disprove it, but it felt so "right." I was content with the idea—I knew for certain that feeling comfortable in my body or in my life was a struggle. But there was a third factor that convinced me all the more. It had to do with three dreams that I'd had between 1972 and 1977, which I had all but forgotten. I had dreamt about beings who looked human, but who had no physical bodies.

These three dreams flashed into my mind after the reading and I wondered: Could these nonphysical beings be archetypal memories from my past deva existence? Could they have been actual communications with devas in my dream consciousness? Do other people dream of nonphysical, etheric beings like these?

Gloria had accurately described my feelings of alienation that I had very seldom talked about. It was true that I experienced the world as a strange place where mothers hurt their children, the strong take advantage of the weak, where money is power, where men oppress women, and women manipulate men. It is a world in which everyone prizes his or her illusions and holds onto them, where television is used to make money instead of to teach and inspire, where being rich is a badge of honor. Millions of people escape from their pain into drug and alcohol addiction. Violent television shows shock people into further indifference.

Along with feeling alienated, however, I also felt simultaneously inferior and superior. In human relationships I feared people's violence, their misuse of power, and I felt inferior and powerless. Gloria said that in past lives I frequently withdrew into convents and monasteries or committed suicide in order to avoid being victimized by violence. I strongly resonated to that. Did I simply lack experience in a physical body?

In this life I had never resorted to violence, and I felt superior for that reason. Even though I was victimized as a child by my mother's verbal violence, it never occurred to me to use violence to gain my own ends. In earlier years my extreme emotional sensitivity was a liability that caused me to feel inferior. The hostility of others caused me intense psychological pain. Hostility directed toward me made me shut down and retreat into a shell. In later years the sensitivity became an advantage. I could "psych people out" and know quickly what psychological game they were playing. I felt closer to divinity than to physical manifestation and could literally feel divine energy within my sensitivity.

Gloria had talked about the deva kingdom as a place of safety and as a place that was not dangerous. I realized that throughout my life I seldom felt truly safe. In my youth, the greatest source of safety had been my father. Somehow his presence, his very being, connected me to a dimension of safety. I realized further that my deepest desire was to find or create for myself the feeling of safety again so that I could be fully myself.

If I were a member of the devic realm, when did I begin to incarnate in the human kingdom? I listened inside and searched psychically for an answer. I had read about the ancient civilizations of Lemuria and Atlantis, but felt no special association with them. However, when I would read or hear about Egyptian and Greek civilizations, I felt an excitement that indicated to me that I had been there. The first time I saw jewelry from the 18th Egyptian dynasty in a museum, for instance, something inside of me recognized it and said, "Yes, I was there." When I studied Aristotle's *Nichomachian Ethics*, I not only felt I knew them previously, but had applied them and lived according to them.

I wanted to find out more about devas so I asked Aniya Glaston. She was a young professional psychotherapist, healer, and channeler of a group of discarnate "light beings." Aniya had frequently been invited by Gabrielle to give workshops at Women and Wisdom. She had a practice in Vermont and regularly came to New York, as she had built up a practice here as well. I felt that I had incarnated into a human body for the first time after the Atlantean era, that is, about ten thousand years ago, and the reading confirmed that.

I asked her how common it was for devas to incarnate in human bodies, and she replied that it was more usual than people might think. She said there are many other planes of existence—other planets, other energies, entities, and many different kinds of beings—who incarnate into the human kingdom. She confirmed what Gloria had said, that when devas incarnated in human form, they were extremely sensitive individuals and sometimes found the pain of trying to incorporate life on the Earth in a human body too much for them. She said that sometimes they died as young children, sometimes they became addicted to alcohol or drugs as a way of escaping this reality, and sometimes they escaped into mental illness. She said that some, but not all people who are addicted or mentally ill are devas. She said that it was very difficult for devas to negotiate in this world for they are used to a kingdom in which there is instant manifestation and where there is no opposition or hostility.

I asked her how many human lifetimes it might take for a deva to become used to human life, and she replied that it could happen in the first incarnation or it may never happen. It also depended on the individual deva's objective and decision. She continued that devas are also some of the greatest healers, thinkers, and leaders that had been upon the Earth. When I asked for examples, she mentioned Albert Einstein and Margaret Sanger.

Gloria, too, had said that the devic dimension was a world without opposition and hostility. How easy it was to imagine such a world. In my inner world there was no hatred or hostility. There was peace, innocence, trust, kindness, approval, support, acceptance, and helpfulness. In my inner world there was no need for protectiveness because there was no danger. There was no need for defensiveness, nor for any pretense. I could be what I am.

In my public world, however, things were different. I was not incapable of such feelings as hostility and hatred, but I did not find them helpful and rarely indulged in them. Whenever I tried to bring my safe inner world into my outer world, I would feel hostile energy come my way and often retreat in fear. Because of my extreme sensitivity, fear was my biggest problem. If I could only get a handle on my fear and act from a place of inner safety, I felt I could be finally myself in the world.

Geoffrey Hodson, a clairvoyant theosophist, wrote in *The Coming of the Angels* that purity, simplicity, directness, and impersonality are four natural characteristics of the angels and that people must develop these qualities also. Angels of high rank possess powers and capacities which human beings have not yet gained, but humans are masters of the physical dimension which they cannot touch. Our voluntary imprisonment here on Earth gives us added knowledge and power, but it costs us our pristine, spiritual purity. The angels retain theirs. They have also kept their sense of the unity of life and are always impersonal and cooperative in everything they do. We, on the other hand, have become personal, separate, and selfish. We can also be devious in going after what we want and make pleasant, but unnecessary detours; the angels waste no time, but go directly to their goals.

Hodson explains that when an angel decides to incarnate into the human kingdom, it is either because of a deep love for a human being or in order to achieve the same mastery of the physical plane as humans have. Angels who are sufficiently evolved to understand human evolution feel reverence and deep respect for the human path of progress through physical matter. From the higher realms, an angel sees the human spirit imprisoned in a body, cramped, limited, weighed down, and blinded by the density of physical matter. Angels know that the human spirit evolves through the physical dimension and one day they will master it. Then they will return to the Father with the most precious gifts gathered from their experience in matter. So, the angels see the glory which shines about human beings on their difficult path.

When an angel contemplates that glory—human spiritual heroism and courage—sometimes it is inspired to tread the same path and win the same prize. Angels, according to Hodson, often regret their decision on their first birth into the human kingdom. Because they have known a freedom which humans have not known, angel souls imprisoned in human flesh suffer more deeply than human souls.

I responded to everything Geoffrey Hodson said about the angels, including that they frequently regret their decision on their first birth into human form. Gloria had said that the first order of business was, of course, to learn how to function on the earth plane. That had not been easy for me, and I had incarnations that were very difficult. When I first came into the human kingdom, I had thought it would be as easy as handing out roses. It had been a big shock to me to discover that the Earth was not necessarily wanting all the sweetness and light I intended to bring it.

At one point I asked Aniya if I had been a particularly weak or stupid deva because, as a human being, I seemed unable to protect myself from violence and aggression. She said that I had made a decision against the use of violence and aggression, and for nonresistance. She did not share my judgment that I was too sensitive and unable to protect myself from violence. "You wouldn't call Gandhi's energy weak or claim that he couldn't protect himself, would you?" No, I would not. Mohandas Gandhi had led the Indian people in the resistance movement against the British government and freed the Indian continent from British rule. Martin Luther King, Jr., had emulated Gandhi's nonviolent ways in the civil rights movement in this country.

Devic energy seemed more feminine to me than average human energy. It seemed natural that I might have a problem with powerful masculine, aggressive, violent energies. Albert Einstein and Margaret Sanger got it right. But how many lives did they have until they got it right? I guess it takes as long as it takes.

Hearing from Gloria and Aniya that I came from the devic kingdom, researching metaphysical sources for more information, and finally accepting that I could be an ex-deva did two things for me. First, I found a beautiful identity to replace the emptiness within, where I had released the negative identity I accepted as a child in Germany. Secondly, this new identity somehow contributed to bring into fruition dormant faculties, such as my intuition, that now began to grow stronger.

Chapter 8
Persistence

> Too long has the entity been, as it were, under a cloud; rather timid, rather lacking in self-expression. It needs to get out in the wilds and yell, and hear its own echo back again.
>
> —(Edgar Cayce reading 3564-2)

DURING 1981 and 1982, the two years I worked at the Lucis Trust, I engaged in a few carefully chosen activities, spending much time listening to music, reading, writing in my journal, and analyzing and working with dream materials. I had sold my car when I moved into Manhattan because finding parking spaces was nearly impossible. When I visited "Uncle John" Spotts in Pennsylvania, I would travel by bus. I spent much time on solitary pursuits, and my thoughts returned to my relationship with my parents that had imprinted on me and "presented me with the karma I had left behind," as Joseph Meade had put it. Gloria had said that my mother had envied me in a past life when we had been sisters, and competitors and I had won because of my sweetness and gentleness. Her power, aggressiveness, and pushiness had not won. She said that my mother, then my sister, had hated me and died hating me, and I had never gotten over being intimidated by her beauty and her power. In this lifetime, however, I had another chance to reexperience her energies and to learn not to be so afraid. She, on the other hand, had another chance to love me by bringing me through her own body.

I felt that I finally had an understanding of the karma that tied me to my mother. I was impressed by the wisdom of God and the Lords of Karma in letting me be born as my mother's daughter. My mother, it seemed, was not some cruel executor of the law of cause and effect; she was actually the perfect teacher to teach me not to be so afraid. When I discussed this issue with a friend, she said, "That makes sense. You don't learn to be fearless by being in a safe surrounding; you learn to be fearless by being exposed to what you consider dangerous, so that you can struggle against it with all you've got on every level and become strong and less afraid, if not fearless and loving."

It was at this point, I think, that I began to detach from my mother in the role of her daughter. I began to see her as an individual soul who was on her own journey back to God. I thought I must have had many lives in which she played no role. She was my mother only in this lifetime and would not be my mother for all eternity. In a spiritual sense, she was my sister and would be my sister for all eternity. Seeing her now as my sister lessened my expectations that she should have been an ideal loving and nurturing mother.

Detaching from my mother was made easier by more forgiveness work. In meditation, I often created an altar of light and put my mother on it. Then I would say, "I forgive you completely for everything you have done to hurt me, real or imagined, in this life or any other, remembered or unremembered, and I ask that you forgive me also." Again I found it enormously difficult to bring into consciousness what I thought she had done to hurt me. Many times I made a list of everything my mother had said that hurt me and forgave her. It helped to regress to the consciousness of the child I once was. I found that the fuller I could reexperience the pain while my heart was filled with forgiveness, the better and more complete was the release. Often my ego resisted and said "enough already," and that it was not important anyway. But I remembered St. Peter asking Jesus, "Lord, how oft shall my brother sin against me, and I forgive him? till seven times? Jesus saith unto him, I say not unto thee, Until seven times: but, Until seventy times seven." (Matthew 18:21)

I was puzzled about why my mother had attacked my femininity, feelings, sensitivity, intuition, and will, but not those of my sisters to the same degree. I asked Aniya about this, and she answered that I was most receptive to the Goddess energy, most in tune with spirit, and I had the most potential for bringing the feminine spirit down into the earth plane. She said that my mother subconsciously sensed this, and it made her jealous because it was an energy with which she had never been comfortable. My energy actually created anxiety and fear inside of her. And so, Aniya continued, my mother organized her energy in such a way to make sure that I would have a very difficult time expressing myself.

That made sense. Psychologists today say that the majority of our communications with each other takes place on a nonverbal level. My mother must have sensed my psychic sensitivity and gentleness shortly after or even before my birth. Being uncomfortable with me to the point of fearing me, she bombarded me with negativity—not so much to hurt me, as to protect herself from my energies.

Because of the forgiveness work I was practicing, my attitude and relationship with my mother became increasingly better. I realized that she was an evolving soul like everyone else. I also realized that I was more than just her daughter—I was the sum total of everything I had done and experienced in all my past lives.

With my new sense of detachment came a stronger feeling of my own identity, and I came to understand that I had been carrying my mother in my head, by the way I "mothered" myself physically, emotionally, and mentally. I saw that the mother character in my dreams was my inner mother: that part of myself that parented me, for good or for ill. My healing efforts were moving me in the direction of healing my inner mother. The following dream of 30 August 1980 made me aware of the lack of love that the mother-in-me had for me.

In the dream, I saw my birdcage with two parakeets and one small parrot in it. I loved these birds very much. My mother came and stuck her hand in the cage, grabbed the birds, and killed them. One even had its wing torn off. I watched it fall to the bottom of the cage. I was enraged and physically felt the heaviness and the power of these emotions.

To get a clearer picture of these two parts of me, I wrote a dialogue between myself and the mother-in-me, following the technique learned from Peter in Gestalt therapy. I put myself into each character in turn with the spiritual knowledge that at the heart of all beings, including the destructive dream-mother, is divine and perfect love.

"I feel rejected," I said, "put down, hurt, and enraged. How could you kill my birds when I love them so much?"

"You?" I asked, playing the part of the mother-in-me. "Your birds? You, love them?"

"Yes," I said. "My birds. Now, why did you kill them?"

"I saw them in the cage," said the dream-mother. "They looked so pretty. It bothered me that they looked so pretty. I wanted them for my own, but I couldn't have them. So I killed them."

"That was a foolish and cruel thing to do," I said. "And it was totally needless. Because you could have enjoyed them with me. You could have gotten pleasure from them, too. Didn't you see that?"

"I am a loser," said the dream-mother. "Good things are not for me."

"Good things are for you, also," I said. "You can enjoy them, too. You are good. You have God inside of you just like anyone else."

At this point in the dialogue, I realized that the dream-mother personified my attitude that I was not good enough and was not entitled to good things. Edgar Cayce spoke frequently about the importance of having the right attitude and ideal. When I worked with my dreams, and especially in dream dialogues, my attitudes that were not in keeping with my ideal became visible. I could then change my thinking. Next I took on the role of the parakeets in my dream and let them speak:

"We are love birds. We are your thoughts of love. We are your aspiration to love. We are your ideas of love. We are also your growing feelings of love. The 'mother-part' of you is uncomfortable with thoughts and feelings of love. She is unfamiliar with love. You must teach her not to reject, repress, or kill love, but to accept it."

Just as I earlier spent many meditation sessions forgiving my mother, now the forgiveness work shifted to forgiving myself. I saw with horror that everything I had accused my mother of doing to me, I had done to myself ever since. Again I made a list and systematically forgave myself, asking God to forgive me, too, for threatening, neglecting, criticizing, insulting, blaming, punishing, and manipulating myself. Every time I did forgiveness work, I actually felt the inner barriers between me and the Divine break down further. I could literally feel divine energy flowing into my personality and strengthening me.

Through this process, I also began to see my father as an evolving soul in his own right with his own individual past and destiny. I often reflected on what Gloria had told me about a past life in ancient Rome when my father had been a teacher of philosophy, teaching only the wealthy and privileged. I had been the son of the cook at the school, a poor, but bright little boy. My father, who usually taught in the open, had not only permitted me to sit on the edge of his class, but had often found excuses to keep me close to him. I had grown up with advanced ideas of philosophy and had later become a public speaker on the rights of women and slaves. This life had continued the positive karma that existed between us already. The love between my father and me had been implicit, and Gloria's depicting of a past life of friendship made perfect sense to me.

I pondered the underlying energies of the many evenings from the age of thirteen to seventeen that followed a pattern. The family had eaten supper and went into the living room to relax. I remained in the kitchen to do the dishes. My father stayed with me, slowly finishing his cup of coffee, smoking a cigarette, and playing with his lighter by turning it over and over on the table. He hardly ever said a word, but sat in silence. His eyes followed my hand as I wiped the table. Often I expected him to act like my mother and critically point out a spot I had missed, but he did not criticize me. He would invariably finish his coffee and his cigarette a few minutes before or after I finished cleaning the kitchen and join the others in the living room. I sensed keenly there was something to be learned from this silent time together, but could not quite put my finger on it. I asked Aniya: "When my father was alive, why did he not speak to me more?"

She answered that he had felt guilty about the way my mother had treated me and that he had done nothing to stop her. He also had a difficult time because he felt an attraction to me and knew it was wrong. As a way to deal with his feelings, he cut himself almost completely off from me.

I asked her if there was a more recent past-life association with him besides the one in ancient Rome when he had been my teacher. She said that just before the turn of this century, we had emigrated together to America from Wales. Once again we were husband and wife. I had become ill on the trip and died shortly after arriving. He had grieved and longed for me. He had called my energy to him again in this life, but was not ready to make a deep commitment because he still felt the pain of that separation. This was another reason why he was so distant.

The information sounded good, and it felt right. But was it true? My heart, guts, and mind responded that this may have happened. It fit my feelings and explained the situation. So, I accepted it and worked with it. Should I discover another truth, I would go with that. There was much in these words that told me I needed to forgive my father, too.

To hasten my healing and growth, I sought out therapeutic groups and activities in Manhattan that were inexpensive or free. A wonderful little newspaper, the *Metropolitan Almanac*, available once a week, listed a myriad of events, especially for single people. That is how I learned about the "Focusing Group" and later the "Morale Group." Both groups met weekly in a professional building on 64th Street and were facilitated by therapists in training. In the Focusing Group we used exercises that combined meditation and psychology from a book by Eugene Gendlin, *Focusing*. The groups were safe places to be with other single people, once or twice a month, to socialize and to learn something new. In the Focusing Group we also did many "listening" exercises. We paired off, and one person told an experience to the other, who then repeated what he or she had understood. When the first person felt satisfied that he or she had been heard, only then could the second person respond.

One night I saw another group meeting next door; it was the Morale Group. I immediately felt connected to the five or six people who regularly attended this group. The object of this group was to raise our overall morale. After a few months, however, our leader left, and the others thought I should replace him. I agreed, reluctantly and excitedly. It was a small group, and I felt comfortable saying what I felt and thought, and I was excited to be the leader.

I no longer let fear stop me from doing what I wanted to do. I would "feel the fear and do it anyway." I also followed up on another one of Edgar Cayce's suggestions and carefully studied the 14th chapter of John. Cayce had said that reading this chapter was the best antidote to fear. I tape recorded the entire chapter and listened to it several times. Often, and especially whenever I felt fearful, I repeated, "Peace I leave with you, my peace I give unto you: not as the world giveth, give I unto you. Let not your heart be troubled, neither let it be afraid." (John 14:27) Taking on leadership of this group was an active step to overcoming my fear.

I changed its name to the "Self-Esteem Group." We gathered once a week, and I opened the group with a go-around in which all members told what was the most loving thing they had done for themselves or someone else during the past week. It could be as big as taking a vacation or as small as getting a haircut. Most people in the group found it difficult to remember to do something loving every week, but they liked coming to the group because this practice encouraged them to think they had the power to do loving things. After the go-around we had open sharing of concerns, problems, accomplishments.

Occasionally I advertised the group in the *Metropolitan Almanac* and usually had about seven or eight people present. One of the regulars was Fred, a retired postal worker and widower with a steady girlfriend. He attended the group every week and said that the group inspired him and made the rest of the week go by easily. Then there were Marty and Joyce, a couple who had been married for thirty years and had difficulties communicating. They liked the group because here was an atmosphere where they could relax. They said it was the only place they went to where they really heard each other.

I was no expert in psychological matters, but my spiritual practices apparently showed. I listened carefully to what everybody said and seemed to impart this skill to the others. I really enjoyed facilitating the group. It was my first experience in accepting authority.

Another group I attended more frequently during this time was an A.R.E. dream group led every Monday night by Leon Van Leeuwen in his apartment on 57th Street. I took many dreams to this group for interpretation. The first reference I made to it in my journal was on February 15, 1982. From my dreams, Leon knew me very well. One day he said, "I don't know anyone else who has experienced as much pain and 'crazymaking' in one's childhood as you and who was not strung out on drugs, addicted to alcohol, or committed to a mental institution." Leon had grown up in a Jewish family in Holland and had a similar upbringing as I did, including an unloving mother. His compliment had meant a lot to me.

The dream group was not only a good place for me to share dreams and receive feedback, but it was a safe place for me to practice speaking up in public. In earlier years I had gone through excruciating pain when speaking to more than one person at a time. Fear of shame and embarrassment had often paralyzed me into silence. Throughout these years I watched my progress in speaking up. I greeted every success with joy, but I was also a hard taskmaster, always expecting more, always pushing.

One of the more active members of Women and Wisdom, Patricia, was an editor. She started a beautiful eight-page newsletter called, of course, "Women and Wisdom." I contributed three short pieces, all focused on the theme of the spiritual woman warrior, which was my way of transforming my victim self into a victor. The last one, published in June 1983, was entitled "A Woman Warrior Is a Winner." In it I wrote, "What is a winner, though? Does it mean that we compete fiercely with others, get all we can for ourselves, and then sit there, hoarding our treasures and showing them off? Not at all. A woman warrior pits herself only against her own past performance. It is not competition that makes a winner. Competitors, unlike warriors, believe there are winners and losers in the world. Competition comes out of self-doubt and feelings of inferiority."

I continued, "Being winning women means giving up our image of ourselves as 'victim.' It has been said that there is a tremendous thought form of 'superior male, inferior female' that envelops our planet. If we are lazy, imitative thinkers, we buy into this thought form and perpetuate in our own lives the female as victim. Let us be creative thinkers. Let us create the path on which we will walk, and let this path be a positive one, full of winning vibrations. Thinking 'I am a winner,' even when we feel weak and vulnerable, *will* create that new thought form. It will push out the old one and soon take over our lives. Winners also look at other women and men as winners and give them credit for what they have achieved. Let's face it: our very nature, our souls, are the stuff that winners are made of."

Reading this article now, I can see how every person I have learned from in this life has contributed to my understanding and made this article possible. When it was published in *Spirit Guide*, I felt happy that I could share with others what I had learned.

Toward the end of 1983, I felt caged by my work at the Lucis Trust. The desire to get a college degree came back very strongly. I knew that some students ran up enormous debts to get their education and then spent years paying it off. That was not an option for me. Whether it was my upbringing or my spiritual path, I could not take out a loan to study. I had learned, however, that free tuition was an employee benefit at most colleges and universities. I decided to get a job at an institution of learning and thus avoid having to pay the thousands of dollars that it would normally cost. Leon cautioned me not to change jobs in order to run away from something unpleasant. "You can't run away," he said. "It'll just follow you and be waiting for you at the next job." I took that advice to heart and searched my mind, but this time I felt that I was not running away from something, but toward something.

How to manifest a position at a university? I decided to spread the word, and the first person I mentioned it to was Maryann, a colleague. Once before I had approached her with a desire. At that time I needed a blender. Maryann had listened and said, "Hmm, what kind of a blender do you want to manifest? I have three at home that I am not using . . ."

This time she also listened. "I have a friend," she said then, "who is a professor at New York University. I believe she is looking for a secretary. Let me talk to her and find out." Sure enough, her friend, Claire, had just accepted a position as professor in the Department of Rehabilitation Counseling at New York University (NYU) and needed a secretary. I contacted her, and a few weeks later, the first week of January in 1983, I began my new job at NYU. It was located on the fourth floor of one of the buildings bordering Washington Square Park. I applied to study at NYU and learned later during the summer that I was accepted for the fall semester to get my bachelor's degree in liberal arts.

Evelyn, a colleague who worked on the sixth floor, told me about a young woman, Shona, who worked on the fifth floor. "She lives in your neighborhood and likes to walk to the office, just like you. You'll have to meet her. Then you two can walk together." Soon after, I was sitting at my desk shortly after the lunch break, when Evy came through the door, pulling a young woman with long blonde hair behind her. "Hi," Evy said, "this is Shona. Shona, this is Jennifer." Evy turned around and left, leaving Shona standing by my desk. The instant my eyes connected with Shona's face, a bright light exploded where the third eye is located. The light was accompanied by feelings of joy, and I intuitively knew that this woman would become my friend. We talked for a few minutes and agreed to meet for lunch so that we could get to know each other.

This time I fully embraced the flashing forth of my third eye as an unusual gift that I had. I felt no fear, only gratitude and excitement. Was this not one of the "gifts of the Spirit" that St. Paul spoke about in his first letter to the Corinthians? "Now there are diversities of gifts, but the same Spirit." (I Corinthians 12:4) I had been blessed with many unusual experiences over the years. Edgar Cayce said about psychic abilities that "There is within every soul the ability to accomplish any influence that has been or may be accomplished in the earth. If the developing of the psychic abilities is meant here—these might be developed, depending upon what the entity seeks as its ideal or as his guide." (Edgar Cayce reading 3083-1) This was the time when I began to appreciate them, but I also remembered, "Though I speak with the tongues of men and of angels, and have not charity, I am become as sounding brass, or a tinkling cymbal." (I Corinthians 13:1)

I found out that Shona came from Alabama. She had been married for seven years, but she seldom referred to her marriage or her ex-husband. She was studying at NYU for her Ph.D. degree in English. She loved poetry and especially Rainer Maria Rilke. One thing we had in common was our love for dreams and symbology. Shona, too, wrote down every dream that she recalled, and she was pretty good at interpreting mine when I felt stuck with one. She was not familiar with metaphysics, and at first she thought I was somewhat strange when I talked to her about Atlantis, reincarnation, and life after death. Soon we fell into a pattern of eating dinner in a restaurant every other month or so and having long, fascinating conversations and sharing our lives with each other.

I thought it was not surprising that Aniya saw positive past-life relationships for us. She said that we had been nuns together in the south of France. Shona had been elderly, a teacher, and I had helped her through her transition from life to death in a way that had benefited us both. That experience had created a special bond between us. In another life, in ancient Greece, she saw us as worshiping together in the temple, dancing in the moonlight, and singing, rejoicing in the love and in the connection of spirit. There were glimmers of that joy in the spirit between us now, she said.

The third connection she saw was as twin sisters in a life as American Indians. She said we blazed trails together and were interested in doing the work of the braves more than that of the squaws. Helping and encouraging each other, we were able to do the things that were not that acceptable or easy to do, but because we had each other, we pursued them and brought them to greater fruition. That was a way in which we could serve each other again in this life, she said.

In July of 1983 I made my first trip to Inwood Park in the northernmost corner of Manhattan, where the Harlem River flows into the Hudson River. I followed an invitation by the park rangers to go on a tour and see places where the raspberries grew. The meeting place was the flagpole. I was there on time, but no rangers showed up. Only a little old man, and we ended up sitting on the bench under the flagpole. We got to talking, and he offered to show me where the raspberries were. He looked gentle and vulnerable and quite safe to be alone with in the park. Also, I had gotten into the habit of "asking" my inner feelings before doing something that might be unsafe or wrong for me to do. As a result of my "asking" I felt a relaxation response and knew I would be safe.

He showed me several places in this wild and uncultivated park where the raspberries grew. Together we picked about two pounds and put them into a bucket I had brought. I wanted to share them with him, but he did not want any. For the next ten years I would return to this park every July to pick raspberries. I explored the park on my own and eventually got to know it very well.

In the fall of that year I began my studies at the Gallatin Division, a school specifically created by NYU for adults. All courses were held in the evenings. I had eighty-two credits from Queens College and The New School for Social Research, and was able to take seventy-one with me to NYU. To graduate, I needed a total of 120 credits, thirty to be taken in the classics—Homer, Aristotle, Plato, Dante, Shakespeare, etc., and I would also have to take a two-hour oral examination with three professors.

With so many credits to start with, graduation seemed just around the corner. At work and in class, I no longer felt like an immigrant, but like a New Yorker. In some classes, especially the very large ones with forty students, I seldom spoke up. But in smaller classes with subjects like Dante, Aristotle, Homer, and especially Shakespeare, I always raised my hand when the professor asked the class a question. Soon I was known for my philosophical bent. I was careful to keep my metaphysical knowledge to myself and to phrase my words in an academic language. I would have loved to say, "Edgar Cayce taught" or "Alice Bailey said," but that would not have been wise.

However, with my adviser, Jim Mirrione, who was not only a professor but also a playwright, I could be more open. When I met with him privately in his office to discuss my schedule, I could be freer and feel safe that he did not pass judgment.

In a class on business communication, taught by Professor Patricia Rock, one of our assignments was to give a ten-minute speech to the class about "something you care about." I wanted to talk about the seven energy centers in the human body and asked the instructor privately if she thought it was appropriate. She supported me in doing it. I had so much material on the seven centers that I decided to limit my presentation to one center only, the one in the heart, the center of love. It was fun to prepare, frightening to anticipate doing, an act of service to do, and glorious to remember that it had gone well. My mouth had been dry, my knees shook, but I did not wet my pants.

In 1983 I connected in a new way with people. I seemed to have a new ability to relate. My head was clearer. I knew what I wanted and what I did not want. I was clearer about what I was feeling. In retrospect, it seemed as if my love feelings for men had stopped when my father died. In the years following his death I dated very little and did not feel passionate love for anyone. I grieved for my father and for the loss of safety that his spirit in the earth had provided for me. Also, I had had to deal with out-of-body experiences and the vivid vision by full consciousness of my own past life as a human sacrifice. Perhaps I had needed these years of inactivity to heal and to regain my balance.

My relationship with Larry had a new tone to it, my contribution to it was brighter, clearer, and surer. With him I did not feel so thin-skinned any more. Larry was divorced and had two teen-age daughters. In those days I tried to live neither in the past, nor in the future, but actively in the present. I did not care much about the future anyway, because I knew it would come soon enough. But the past kept intruding. I felt safe with Larry, and I felt that I knew him from before. I felt safe enough to talk about past lives, but he did not take it seriously and joked about what he might have been. One night I had a clear feeling that he had been my son in an American Indian incarnation and I had lost him.

A little while later I dreamt that I saw a funeral pyre on which my husband, Larry in another life, was being burned. I, the widow, looked at the burning pile of wood and bush and chose the place for me. To this spot I would climb and be burned to death. Thankfully, this dream did not have intense emotions connected with it. Perhaps I had been his wife in India, where widows were expected to climb on their husband's funeral pyre and die themselves so that they would not be a burden to their families.

Little things, like the feeling that Larry had been my son and the dream that he had been my husband, happened often during these years in various relationships. A part of my mind looked backward into the past. I felt enormously enriched by these tidbits from past lives, especially since they came without my having to do anything. In spite of, or perhaps because of, past-life connections, my association with Larry was not shaping up as I would have liked. I could not get a restful night's sleep with him beside me. My passion had reawakened with him, and I wanted the pleasure of sleeping next to him the whole night, waking up together, and sharing breakfast. But I could not find the peace it takes to fall asleep.

Sinking intuitively into these feelings, I detected that my lack of peace was a response to something that was going on within Larry's unconscious mind. Whatever it was, it made me feel rejected by him on a very deep but unconscious level. I wanted to be wanted, consciously as well as unconsciously. I discussed it with him, but he felt powerless to do anything about it.

I thought perhaps another dream I had about Larry might explain it. I had dreamed that Larry's mother had knocked him unconscious and thought that her dream behavior symbolized how she treated him in childhood. She was a woman who wore heavy make-up and had many artificial feelings. Larry, I thought, had never recovered from his childhood. One night when I was unsuccessfully trying to fall asleep beside him, I said out loud, "I really think that deep down you don't want me to be here." Instead of assuring me that he wanted me there, he chuckled. I said it again, and he said, "You don't have to keep on saying it." It was true then.

Unconsciously he was rejecting me. It was strange because consciously he loved me, wanted me, and had previously expressed fear that I would leave him. He rejected me because he was afraid. He also could not deal with my psychic perceptions of his feelings. I could not adjust to the unconscious rejection, and he felt that he could not change. I felt angry and hurt. For a while our relationship limped along. We enjoyed each other's company but spent nights in our separate apartments. When we eventually broke up, my body went into mourning, shutting down, and I was unable to eat for several days.

In May 1984 I signed up for my second workshop at the A.R.E. in Virginia Beach, "The Power of Love in Relationships." Gerald Jampolsky, Gay Luce, Carol Bush, and Charles Thomas Cayce (Edgar's grandson) were some of the presenters. I arrived at the Marshall's Motel just in time for dinner.

At eight o'clock there was an orientation at the A.R.E. During the "getting to know you" exercises I talked at length with the most handsome, gentle, smart, and loving young man there. He told me he was newly divorced, had two children, and was planning to study at the Union Theological Seminary in New York for the priesthood. He looked to me as if he belonged in a church and as if he had spent many previous lifetimes in monasteries. I nicknamed him the "monk." In the singles' group in the afternoon, I kept an eye on the "monk," but I did not choose him as a partner for any of the exercises, nor did he choose me.

The conference turned out to be very exciting. I felt much less shy than the last time I had attended a conference. I felt I had interesting things to say and connected easily with people. I even spoke up in workshops, asked questions, and felt unashamedly proud of myself for doing so. Once again I joined a sharing group comprised of other conference members. Mary, a woman my age from Florida, and Dorothy, a lovely white-haired lady, were also in this group. Dorothy had many past-life memories and astral projection experiences. She told me her memories and I told her mine. The sharing group met each day after lunch.

One day Dorothy complained about her eye, which had a burst blood vessel. Diane, our group leader, asked me to help raise the energy level in the room by leading the group in chanting before doing some healing on Dorothy's eye. I had discussed chanting, my recent spiritual discipline, with Diane. We did three chants, "Lord Jesus Christ, Son of God, have mercy on me, a sinner," "One with all life, Holy I am," and "Gloria in Excelsis Deo." Diane thought the energy level in the room was very high afterward and credited it largely to the chanting. I was glad that the chanting was successful and that I was able to be a channel of blessings to others. She then worked on Dorothy's eye until Dorothy felt better. Everybody was relaxed and remained quiet for a while.

We spent Wednesday morning listening to Gay Luce lecture and asking her questions. After lunch, about 100 other conferees and I sauntered into the auditorium and plopped down in our seats. We were full of food, warm from the sun, and waited to be taught and entertained. Gay came in and took the microphone. She asked if we would go out into the hall and enter the auditorium once more.

We lined up behind her as she held a large vase with fresh flowers. On cue, the audio technician played a piece of music Gay had previously instructed him to play, "Greek Odes," ancient Greek lyrics set to music by Vangelis and sung by Irene Papas. One moment we had stood, bored conferees, wanting to be taught and entertained, and the next moment, surrounded and filled with sacred music, we were transformed into holy supplicants. We moved our holy feet and our holy bodies in a sacred procession, following Gay into the auditorium as if it were an ancient, sacred, healing temple dedicated to the god Asclepius in ancient Greece.

In a part of my mind I saw a scene of white, rocky cliffs above a warm, friendly ocean and felt a mild, healing breeze from the water. We seemed surrounded by holiness and devotion as we opened ourselves to receiving the divine energy of healing. We moved our holy bodies among rows of holy seats in the holy auditorium. We gently lowered our holy bodies into the seats. We took holy breaths and looked with holy eyes at a holy Gay Luce. She told us that some historians believe that the ancient Greeks honored the god Asclepius in this way when they led a procession into one of his healing temples.

I was haunted by the sounds of Irene Papas's voice the way one is haunted by something divine, until I eventually succeeded in tracking down the recording in New York. Even now, when I listen to it, I feel as if I am within a hair's breath of a pool of memories that have to do with Greece, sound, and healing.

On Friday evening we had a social wine and cheese party. The "monk" was not there. On Saturday I lay in the sun on the beach until eleven. Then I cleared out my room, turned in my key, and waited in the A.R.E. Bookstore for the bus to the airport. I was early, so I talked with the people I knew, then spotted the "monk" at the other end of the store. Our eyes met, and he came over to talk with me. We chitchatted about the conference. I am usually unable to make small talk, but with the "monk" it was easy. Then we went our separate ways.

A few hours later I boarded a Piedmont airlines plane in Norfolk at the same time as my friend, the "monk." He suggested we sit together during the flight. The starry-eyed Juliet within me excitedly realized that she would be spending a whole hour with her handsome Romeo. What good luck! Meanwhile, another part of my mind wondered: Why did God arrange it this way?

For an hour we shared our lives with each other. I learned more about him, and he asked me about my life. We enjoyed an hour of emotional honesty and intimacy in a rare state of spiritual unity flying in the airplane above the clouds. We shared our disappointments and our hopes. We grew serious. We laughed. It was as if we had left our personalities on the ground and taken only our soul bodies with us on the plane. Nothing marred that hour of perfect love and sharing. I had a delightful time being near him, looking at his boyish face with its clear, bright smile, and I thought I detected just a shadow of bewilderment there. We parted at Newark airport with a hug and with each other's addresses and phone numbers in our pockets, intending to meet soon.

I had a weekend to spend before returning to work. My mind was obsessed with the "monk." Emotionally, I was heartsick with infatuation for him, but during meditation, when I thought I had freed myself from that emotional desire, I felt a pure, unconditional love for him. On the airplane, I had sensed that he felt the same way. Through meditation, I got myself calmed down enough to realize that if anything were going to happen between us, it would be God's will.

Still high and in touch with divine energy from the conference, I created a personal chant and used it that weekend to get over "the monk" and also used it many years later in my personal healing work. The chant consisted of three notes, repeated seven times. The words to the chant came into my conscious mind from a higher place. I chanted: "I love you" (7x); "You are free" (7x); "You love me" (7x); "I am free" (7x). The desire and fear energy that had been stuck in my three lower chakras was lifted up to my heart chakra, where it was transformed and lost all negativity. The chanting freed me from my obsessive romantic attachment and brought me a precious dream the following night in which I believe I came face to face with my soul or higher self.

In the dream, I had just come back from a vacation by the ocean. I liked it so much that I made plans to spend my next vacation also by the ocean. My Higher Self held me in her arms and flew with me through the air. She suggested that next time I spend some time in the woods and mountains. She pointed out several places that were possibilities for me to choose from. I felt infinitely safe being carried in her arms. I still felt the desire to be at the ocean again, but if she thought the woods were a better place, I would check it out. I looked at her face directly in front of me. She looked exactly like me! She had my chin, cheeks, nose, forehead, and eyes. But her spirit was different. There was no tension in her face. She looked relaxed, at ease. She looked incapable of feeling stress. She looked—and I knew she was—perfect in every way. I surrendered to her wisdom and love, like a much-wanted child.

In the following weeks, I was in touch with the "monk" by telephone a few times with hopeful anticipation. We wanted to set up a meeting to see each other, either in New York or where he lived, which was not far away. However, we never met. I felt sad, but I surrendered my will to God. I was grateful that he had played a role in the love and joy I received from sound and in coming face to face with my soul.

I had been first introduced to working with Edgar Cayce's concept of ideals in 1980 at an A.R.E. conference in Virginia Beach. "An ideal is something beyond and above us toward which we build . . . From the physical, mental, and spiritual viewpoints our ideals are patterns by which we endeavor to shape our lives." (*A Search for God*, Book I) At the time I could not fully understand how I could work with them. Setting an ideal is essentially setting a purpose. Edgar Cayce said:

> Analyze self and the purposes, the motives, the influences; and know that they agree with that which is thy ideal. What is thy ideal? Spiritually, mentally, physically? Not what you would wish God to do for you, but what may you do in appreciation of the love shown? Not as to what ye would like to be, but what may ye mentally give that will be conducive to constructive thinking in the experience of others? In the physical, not what you want others to do for you, but what may you do for them? (Edgar Cayce reading 1995-1)

At the conference in 1984, ideals were mentioned again, and this time the idea took root in my mind. We were handed sheets of paper with three circles of different sizes, one within the other. The outer two were divided into quarters. Into the center circle we were to put our spiritual ideal, into the middle the mental, and into the outer the physical. I photocopied the sheet and worked on my ideals off and on for years until thinking in those terms became second nature.

Edgar Cayce suggested that the ideal be set in positive words. I had a great deal of trouble at first doing that because my mind was thinking in negatives, "I don't want this, I don't want that." Eventually, however, I learned to focus on positive values. I wanted to overcome fear, but that was not an ideal. The ideal was the opposite of fear, namely confidence, courage, love, and joy. I put CONFIDENCE in the center circle.

Now I needed to find the "ideal" mental attitude that expressed the ideal of CONFIDENCE in my relationships to my work, hobbies, friendships, and myself. I struggled through my fuzzy thinking about my true values. Then I asked myself what activities follow naturally from those mental attitudes? These would be activities that expressed confidence and would lead to more confidence. I put them in the outer circle marked "physical." I found that the statements I eventually placed on the diagram were not so very important. The important thing was the process of thinking through, contemplating, and weighing what was important to me.

Out of this ideals work came one particular ideal that helped change my attitude toward authority, namely, "I want to serve with honor." This simple statement put my mind in the right place regarding my age-old problem with authority. Cayce often repeated that attitudes are important, and so I had begun to pay attention to my attitudes toward authority figures. I had occasionally experienced difficulties with this, especially when a person in authority abused his or her power. I am sure that having had one parent who assumed no authority and the other who abused it had something to do with this, although I also believed that I carried a distrust with me from past lives in which I believe I was victimized by people in authority.

Michelle, a strong woman not yet thirty years old and my colleague since my promotion to the office of the president at New York University, added a fresh dimension to my new attitude toward authority. Even when Dr. Brademas, president of NYU, left her a tape with two dozen requests in one day—which happened—she kept her cool and never criticized. She would say with a laugh, "What Dr. Brademas wants, Dr. Brademas gets." Her attitude made her relationship with him simple. She knew him well, trusted and admired him. From then on I incorporated that particular attitude into my own that I had come to trust. The ideals work was also, I thought, training in my desire to do God's will. Confidence in my own judgment that God is trustworthy is a prerequisite to trusting Him.

In the summer of 1985 I discovered a new church, Unity. I had attended services at a Lutheran church in Manhattan, but I really did not feel at home there, nor could I speak openly without suppressing my feelings and experiences. At Unity it was different. Unity was founded nearly 100 years ago, and the members call themselves "students" of Unity. Unity students accepted self-healing, reincarnation, and—very important to me—the natural innocence of every human being.

My graduation from college approached, and the two-hour oral examination was scheduled for February 1986. I had chosen Jim Mirrione, my adviser, and Patricia Rock and Bella Mirabella, my favorite instructors, as the examining professors. I had prepared a list of some twenty classical books that I "professed proficiency in" and would be questioned about. This oral examination, an unusual requirement for an undergraduate degree, was meant more as a valuable experience for the student from which to learn than as a tough exam to put one on the spot. During the exam I relaxed and had fun and went a little too far into metaphysical areas. My adviser told me later that the three of them had discussed afterward how, throughout the exam, they had to keep asking questions to bring me back from the metaphysical to the academic point of view. But I had done well, nonetheless, and passed.

In April, I received a letter from the Gallatin Division that informed me that I had been named a university honor scholar because my grade-point average was 3.5. The letter invited me to an honors scholars' celebration. Walking home that evening near Gramercy Park, I saw Shona a block ahead of me and hurried to catch up with her. We entered the Gramercy Park Hotel to celebrate and have refreshments. When we previously had dinner together, we often argued heatedly about metaphysical and religious ideas, but that day our conversation was especially friendly, sisterly, and intimate. She was happy for me and congratulated me.

But while walking home, in spite of the celebratory mood, I dove into my self-pity and said to Shona, "Just imagine where I could be in my life if I had had loving and caring parents who had encouraged me. I could be a doctor, maybe a famous and successful Jungian analyst. Or a professor, teaching metaphysics at some university."

"You are one of the kindest, sweetest, most interesting and compassionate people that I have ever met," said Shona. "If you had had loving and caring parents, you may have been a successful professional individual, but chances are you would also have become a selfish and ungrateful person. I think you were very lucky that you had the parents you had. They were exactly right for you. They helped make you into the wonderful person that you are." She convinced me, and I thought that she was probably right.

On the afternoon before the honors celebration, Michelle asked me if I wanted her to "sneak" a line about me into the speech Dr. Brademas was to deliver that evening. I thought she was joking and said, "Sure." But in the evening, while sitting with three other honors students from the Gallatin Division, Dr. Brademas said, "... and it gives me great pleasure that one of the students we are honoring here tonight is a member of my personal staff, Jennifer Borchers ... " My schoolmates looked at me with surprise, "Is that you?" I nodded, smiled, and felt like bursting into bloom.

The ceremony for the rest of the 1986 NYU graduating

class was held in Washington Square Park on June 5. I was forty-two years old. I had bought four tickets and invited Tina and her husband Tom, and two friends. Wearing my black cap and purple gown, I felt as if I had finally made it into social acceptability. The now late Senator Thomas "Tip" O'Neil was the commencement speaker. When the ceremony in the park was over, I took my little group up to the twelfth floor to show them where I worked. My colleagues had already left for the day, and suddenly Dr. Brademas came out of his office, warmly greeted my little group, and took them into his office to show them the view over Washington Square Park. They were delighted. In the evening, we celebrated by seeing the Broadway play "Cats" and had dinner in Rolf's, a German restaurant that served a fantastic sauerbraten with potato dumplings.

Chapter 9
Rapture

Was it therefore that our bosoms pin'd?
Were we in the light of suns now dead,
In the days of rapture long since fled,
Into One united?
—(*The Mystery of Reminiscence*, by Friedrich Schiller)

A few days after graduation in 1986, after a hiking trip in the Bronx Botanical Garden, I noticed two young men hanging around the edge of our group, talking to each other. One of the young men later appeared at the station where I waited for the Metro North train to New York City. "Weren't you part of that group?" he asked politely, curiously. He was clean and healthy looking, six feet tall, broad shoulders, with an open and honest face and dark brown hair. His name was Brian.

He sat beside me on the train, talking, all the way to Grand Central Station. As we stepped off the train, he invited me to share a cup of coffee in a little shop in the station to continue our talk, and I accepted. He told me he was

Irish-American and lived across the river in New Jersey. He had two years of college and worked at a large insurance company downtown. He carried a paperback edition of an English translation by the French author Marcel Proust and said he loved literature and hoped to write books himself some day. When I got ready to leave, he said, "What do you think of me?"

"You're a nice young man," I said. His eyes lit up, and I thought I knew what he was thinking. "But you're too young for me," I said, "and I'm too old for you for any kind of romance. How old are you anyway?"

"I am twenty-six," he said. People usually guessed my age as ten or more years younger than I really am. Spiritually I felt ancient, but emotionally I didn't feel much older than twenty-two.

"Seventeen years' age difference," I said. "That would not work."

"But could we be friends?" he asked.

"Maybe," I replied.

"Then, may I call you next week?" he asked.

Brian called, and on the following Saturday afternoon we walked through a block party in my neighborhood, sat on a stoop, and ate slices of watermelon. We met a few more times, like friends, sharing bits and pieces of our lives, enjoying each other's company. We sat on a bench by the East River near the Water Club and watched the moon rise and cast a long avenue of moonlight over the water. I tried not to think romantically about my new friend. But then a festive yacht landed right in front of us, and a wedding party got off. This stimulated my romantic feelings, so, in order to keep myself under control, I said: "Moonlight used to affect me, but it doesn't do anything for me any more."

Suddenly, however, we became very quiet and said little as he walked me home. The next day he called and expressed his feelings. "I know you said we could only be friends, but I feel more than friendship for you. I want to be with you. Will you please reconsider? Can we be lovers?" I had spent the morning reconsidering and simply said, "Yes, we can be lovers." I had come to think that ours was not a chance meeting. In spite of the age difference, I felt an inner urge to open my heart to Brian and enter into an intimate relationship with him.

He suggested a visit to the Tibetan Museum in Staten Island the following Saturday. That afternoon, spent in the secluded and sacred Tibetan Museum garden, was one of infinite emotional tenderness and sweetness. We were shielded by a high fence on one side and had a view into the far distance on the other. There were stone statues of Tibetan holy men, stone elephants, and a water basin frequented by little birds.

When he kissed me for the first time, he seemed a bit bashful and in awe that his wish was coming true. I experienced a special timeless magical feeling and felt again that it was right for me to love this man in spite of the age difference. When we left the museum, he held my hand all the way home. We walked from the Staten Island ferry to 35th Street, stopping in a park where music played, sitting on the grass under a tree to listen. Brian said: "Can I really make love to you tonight?"

I assured him, yes, we would make love and he could spend the night with me. He was not inexperienced, but there was an innocence in him that was rare. From then on we spent all of our weekends together. Often he came directly from work on Friday night and stayed until Monday morning. His love, to me, was a gift from the gods. His easy physicality was utterly healing to me. In spite of the age difference, there was a feeling of equality and of oneness between us that I had experienced only once before—with Franz-Heinz.

Very early in our relationship I attended the A.R.E. family

camp near Roanoke, Virginia, for the second time. While there, I wrote Brian a letter about my "wild and crazy passion" for him and asked if he was sure that he really wanted me. In his letter he wrote that he had the same "wild and crazy passion" for me and, yes, he really wanted me.

While at the camp that week, from morning until night in the company of spiritually oriented people, I thought about my new relationship and talked to God about it in my prayers and meditations. When I had turned forty, I thought there would be no more romance for me. Here I was, forty-two years old, in love with a handsome twenty-six-year-old man. Was it the French writer, George Sand, who had a relationship with a man seventeen years her junior? I discovered that every relationship in my life had a purpose, and I reflected on the purpose for which God sent this young man to cross my path.

Edgar Cayce often advised people to set an ideal for their lives or for portions of their lives. I could choose an ideal for my relationship with Brian and give it form, shape, and purpose. I decided my main objective would be *to love him.* I was aware of many other ideals I could have chosen—to learn, to have fun, to be loved—but I chose to love him. There were times when it was blissfully easy to love him, and there were times when it was a challenge.

We both loved nature and parks more than anything else and were happiest out of doors. We visited Central Park many times. We took subway rides to parks in the other boroughs, the Bronx, Queens, Brooklyn, and Staten Island. Shortly after 4 July weekend, I asked him to come with me to pick raspberries at Inwood Park, in the uppermost corner of Manhattan Island where the Harlem River flows into the Hudson River. An old friend of mine, Fred, also came along to pick berries for his girlfriend. For many hours we picked our way through thick bushes which clung to our clothes, collecting a total of three gallons of berries. Then we sat on a rock on the path and ate the sandwiches I brought. Brian disappeared. When he returned, he said, "Come with me, I want to show you something," and he led me by the hand to a big old beech tree. He had carved our initials into the bark.

"No one has ever done that for me," I said.

"It's the first time I've ever done it," he replied.

We got the raspberries to my kitchen, where we cleaned them from leaves, twigs, and little black bugs. The bugs were as eager to get out of the berries as we were to get them out. Unlike Brian who grew up eating store-bought food all his life, I grew up in the country and was used to cutting a live worm out of an apple before eating it and picking caterpillars off kale before bringing it into the kitchen for washing and cooking. With exaggerated horror, Brian picked the bugs off the berries and shuddered at the thought of accidentally eating even one tiny insect. "Don't worry," I teased, "it won't hurt you; it's extra protein."

After our meal that night, we had big dishes of vanilla ice cream topped with fresh raspberries. In the morning I made waffles with fresh raspberries. After he left my apartment, I got my raspberry picking gear together and took the A-train back to Inwood for some serious picking. Over the past years I explored the entire park and knew just where the berry bushes were. Many narrow and winding paths crisscrossed the park; at first I got lost and wandered around until I found my bearing. The wide Hudson River to the west was the best landmark. In previous years I had occasionally taken a friend along to pick berries, but usually I went alone and enjoyed the solitude under the trees.

Over the years I had developed the "art of raspberry picking." I wore a pair of old running shoes, an old pair of pants with pockets and a belt, a long-sleeved shirt, and head covering. I packed my red nylon backpack with two empty plastic one-gallon water bottles with the tops cut off but the handles left on, one empty quart container, a sandwich, water bottle, and sometimes my camera.

Arriving at the first patch of berries, I put my backpack in a spot where I could easily find it again, inserted my belt through the handle of the quart container so that I had both hands free for picking. Then I faced the luscious raspberries all around and went slightly bananas. The abundance of Mother Nature overwhelmed me every time. Wherever I looked, raspberries by the handful. Just for the picking. Totally free. My greed showed and I gave in to it. I would start picking as if I were obsessed. With both hands I picked and dropped the berries into the container that hung from my waist. I felt feverish. I wanted these berries, I wanted them all, I didn't want anybody else to get them, I had to get them before somebody else came and picked them.

By the time the quart container was half full, my madness subsided. I slowed down. My feelings changed from greed to gratefulness. Mother Nature was so generous. The berries were so beautiful. As I walked farther away from the path and deeper into the patch, I was overcome by feelings of gratitude. "Holy Mother," I would say, "thank you for letting these berries grow here. Thank you for your abundance. Thank you for your generosity."

Then I would become aware of the birds singing in the trees and wild flowers blooming around me on the ground. I realized that I could never pick all the berries in this park. When I met other berry pickers, I greeted them and chatted about the state of the berries this year. Several years in a row I met a Russian man who picked berries for his wife. There was also a Japanese woman who knew nature—not only berries, but also herbs for healing. And there were families who lived close by who came to pick berries from the paths. When my quart container was full, I returned to my red backpack and emptied the berries into one of the gallon containers. Then I returned to the patch. If I had seen poison ivy near me, now would be the time to rub my hands and face with the juice of the jewel weed, a natural antidote to poison ivy, that grew among the raspberry bushes.

Filling the two gallon containers with berries took about three to four hours. Then I tried to be near the Overlook Rock, high above the Hudson River, to eat my lunch. My hands and wrists were scratched, and I would be hot. Beside me stood twelve quarts of fresh raspberries. In the city, a pint of raspberries cost $2.50. I was rich. After lunch, I lifted the heavy backpack and set out for the A-train and home.

I joked to Brian that I had made everything out of raspberries except a new winter coat. I have made jam and jelly. The jelly was great on bread and in jelly rolls. I have made syrup and served fresh raspberries over vanilla ice cream and over yogurt. Raspberry sauce is terrific in the morning over cereal or over pancakes. I have even made raspberry wine.

When Brian spent the weekend at my apartment, he always helped with the cooking and dish washing. When we were not walking hand in hand through nature or sleeping together, we worked together in the kitchen. This was always reason for laughter because New York studio apartment kitchens are so small. Two people have to love each other to function there. We were like two mad cooks, running in and out, reaching over, under, behind, and in front of each other.

When we could not be out of doors, we watched nature shows on television, lay arm in arm on the bed, or played board games. After making love, we would fall asleep for an hour and awaken to find our limbs on top of one another, intertwined, or our feet on the pillow. We slept together like two little puppy dogs. It was the most remarkable thing, as if our bodies were not separate from each other but joined together. Brian had no inhibitions about any part of his body, which was handsome anyway and could have been used by Michelangelo as a model for his "David." But he also thought my body was as beautiful as his.

My ideal to "love him" meant that I would endeavor to keep my heart open to him, to be aware of his feelings, and not do or say things that would hurt him. It meant I would accept him the way he was and not desire to change him. However, it did not mean that I would stop loving myself or sacrifice my needs for him. I wanted to take care of myself as much as I wanted to love him. One night I lay beside him in bed and suddenly felt a strong sense of fear, which might have been because of a bad dream that I did not remember. Moving closer to him, I said, "Please hold me, I'm afraid." Half asleep, he put his arms around me, pulled me closer, and said, "I've got you now." I felt comforted and safe.

My feelings for Brian resembled my feelings for Franz-Heinz, and it was uncanny. I actually wondered if they could have been one and the same soul. Was Brian the reincarnated Franz-Heinz? But no, that could not be since Brian had been born six months before Franz-Heinz died.

During our first summer together, Brian asked me to marry him. I was flattered, but my intuition told me marriage would not work for us. I suggested we wait and see how we got along after a year or two. Shortly afterward, we were sitting on a bench in a children's zoo. It was another magical day. Why did we go to the children's zoo? We were both adults, but we enjoyed sitting on the bench and watching parents and their children go by. We threw coins into a little fountain, and suddenly I wished to marry him. For about twenty minutes marriage seemed like a good idea and that we could be happy as a married couple. But my intuition came back strongly saying, no, and I retracted my wish.

Brian did not easily reveal the facts of his life. It took a while for me to find out that he was born in November of 1960 and was a Scorpio like me. His father had been an active alcoholic throughout Brian's childhood. When he was twelve, he realized his father's negative influence on the family, his mother, his sister, and himself, and he asked him to leave. His father was a gun-carrying security guard and threatened him with his weapon, an act which traumatized Brian and gave him a fear and hatred for weapons. His parents eventually divorced, and his mother soon developed cancer and died at age forty-two. These external circumstances of his life were important, but I cared just as much about our inner connection. So I made an appointment with Aniya Glaston to explore them psychically. I arrived at Aniya's with some questions already prepared.

"Last March I dreamed of Franz-Heinz who died twenty-five years ago," I said. "It seems that he came into my dream to tell me that soon there would be someone whom I would love as much as I had loved him. Brian is very much like Franz-Heinz, and I wonder if there is any kind of a connection between these two souls?"

"Yes, there is," Aniya said. "I get two feelings about it. One is a very strong one of brotherliness, not biological brothers, but spiritual brothers. Their souls are connected, belonging to the same group. It's not unusual for that to happen. It is as if they were relay runners in your life, Franz leaving and handing the baton and his legacy to Brian, who is going to do the next part."

"I feel sure," I said, "that I have known Brian in a previous life. Can you tell me what kind of relationship we had?"

"I see a very ancient life," she said. "It almost doesn't feel like this realm, and I think it wasn't, but I don't know exactly how to describe it."

Intuitively I sensed what she had perceived. An ancient life "not of this realm" could only mean that we were together in the deva kingdom. Was that the connection among the three of us? Had Franz-Heinz also come from the deva kingdom? The energy felt right. I asked if the energy she felt could be that of the deva kingdom.

"Yes," she said, "it was a different place, a different realm. The devas, that makes sense, because there is much nature energy in the two of you. You both operate from a different basis than most. You also had other incarnations together since then," she continued. "The earlier connection, though, overrides any incarnation and is a very strong, powerful, and extraordinary bond. I also see the two of you having assisted each other in major transitions. You both had the experience, this is kind of interesting," she chuckled, "of having assisted at the birthing, literally, physical birthing, of the other."

She said that she also saw us together in a life that seemed to have much fear in it. We were running from an enemy. She said we were both healers and mates. She felt the group that we belonged to had been overthrown, and we had to escape because they were trying to kill everyone in that group. We were trying to escape over a mountain. They had almost caught up with us, I had gone on ahead, and he had been killed. She said that I had made it to the other side and there I birthed a son. I had taught my son the skills I had, and he went on to continue the teaching. Other people of our group who had survived congregated around him. She said that the energy felt like a Brian-to-Franz feeling, as if Brian handed the baton of his relationship to me to this other soul, Franz, who became Brian's child.

Aniya's reading stretched my credulity to the breaking point, and I am not sure if I really believe it. But it was possible. "There are more things in Heaven and earth, Horatio, Than are dreamt of in your philosophy," said Hamlet (act 3, scene 5, lines 166-167). It was possible that the unusual connection between Franz-Heinz and me existed because he, too, came from the deva kingdom. He was not jealous that I loved another man because his love for me was on a soul level and not on a personality level. If Brian's origin were also in the deva kingdom, this could explain why I felt he were my twin soul. Even felt that our physical bodies were made of the same stuff. Our love for nature, it seems, had its roots in our devic origin.

Aniya said that Brian had helped me to get born once and I had helped him. My own psychic feelings neither confirmed nor denied this. But when I recalled her saying that we had been healers and mates and on the run, I received mental images in which I saw us together in southern Europe, either Greece or Turkey, before there were any cities or paved roads. We were very much connected then and dependent on each other.

What a tale, though, that many lifetimes ago Franz had been my and Brian's son! It was all so fantastic! Could Aniya have been making it up? My psychic sense corroborated what she said, that there was a loving and noncompetitive connection among our three souls. We three seemed to share an honesty and truthfulness in expressing our energies to the world. We seemed to share morality and ethics and a lack of experience on the earth plane that made us vulnerable to those who take advantage of the defenseless.

More and more Brian showed up late for our dates. He said it was not lack of consideration for me, but that he refused to wear a watch. His lateness infuriated me and made me feel neglected and unimportant. One Saturday morning, we had hot croissants for breakfast and got into another one of those disagreements that was painful and frightening, but which also helped us understand each other. We had been in that emotional place so many times that I no longer regretted it; it was like going to the cellar, finding out what's down there, and cleaning it up. What was down there, of course, were the monsters of the subconscious, the heads of the hydra, but now I was seeing them on a different turn of the spiral. After breakfast we dressed for the park without resolving our disagreement.

Before leaving, though, I went into the bathroom and while alone in there for a minute, remembered a comment made by Gerry Jampolsky during his lecture at the A.R.E.: "Love brings up all things unlike itself." Loving Brian was bringing up fear in me from a deeper layer of my psyche. I asked the inner wisdom what to do at this very moment and received the guidance to simply be loving. So, I emerged in a conciliatory mood and told Brian that I didn't mean to give him a hard time. Disarmed, he put his arms around me and held me close and said, "Why do you get scared so easily?" I was amazed that he caught on to my fear and could accept it. I still felt my terror of power deeply and sobbed into his warm brown sweater. I told him that I was scared of power and that he had a lot of it, physically, emotionally, and intellectually. He seemed to have no fear of power. I said that I had seen power misused so often and that that fear was still with me; that when I was in my right mind I did not fear him, but trusted and loved him. He replied that he understood, kissed me, and said that he loved me, too. And then we went off to Central Park, feeling good.

I loved him better (not more) than I had ever loved anyone. I felt more loved by him than by anyone else. I felt such a deep connection with him, it went beyond age and beyond our bodies. I felt happy when I was with him, even when we disagreed, and I felt depressed when I was apart from him. With him I felt like the first woman and he felt to me like the first man. I could show him my joy and I could show him my fear. He trusted me with his despair, his anger, and his dreams. We were not together by accident. I was sure we had made an agreement to be together before we were born. I only wished I knew more of the particulars of that agreement.

Eventually, Brian told me that he needed "space." I was clear when I told him that I would give him as much space as he wanted. I still loved him passionately, but my chosen ideal was, however, to *love him* and, therefore, I would not allow myself to go against his wishes. This ideal of loving him gave me a certain amount of detachment. Even though he finally left and put distance between us, I could still love him. I would not lose the pleasure of feeling the special feelings of love I had for him. We saw less of each other, met only occasionally, and kept in touch by phone. At this time I did not hurt nor did I blame myself. Perhaps I knew deep down that our relationship was not yet finished, that we would have one dance to dance with each other in the future.

His pulling away from me unfortunately marked the beginning of a difficult time for him. First, he lost his job and then his apartment. He became extremely critical of everything. He flew to Florida to stay with his grandmother and hoped to find a job there. He called periodically, but I had mixed feelings about his calls. On one hand I wished to be finished with this relationship, while on the other hand, since we had this deep connection and since I had set the ideal of loving him, I wanted to keep my heart open and remain friends.

Meanwhile, I was busy pursuing my own interests. When I obtained my B.A. degree from New York University in 1986, I felt very grateful that the universe, or God, had made this possible for me. Graduation made me think of my brother Richard in Germany. Born in 1949, he had finished grammar school at the age of fourteen, but could neither read nor write. He got a job at the sawmill, the same one that had been targeted but missed by a bomb during the war. He was a good worker and also liked cars and motors. When he was eighteen, he built himself a car from parts that he had found or that were given to him by people in the village. Since he had no license, he could not drive on public roads, but only on private paths between fields and meadows. He very much wanted a license.

Richard asked our brother Johann to read the drivers' manual to him so that he could memorize it. He obtained permission to take the written test orally and passed. He got his license. Soon he bought himself a new car. Once, when I visited, I sat with him several times and tried to teach him to read, but I could not. He seemed to have something similar to dyslexia. Together with my mother, we made arrangements for him to attend special classes in Bremerhaven with other illiterate adults. Richard was the only student who arrived at the school driving a car. He finally learned to read and write passably by the age of twenty-eight.

I thought of Richard in 1986 when I saw a notice in the back of a book stating that the New York Public Library system needed volunteers to teach literacy skills to adults. Reading and writing had come to me without effort, and I felt I had something to give. I also felt guilty because intellectual pursuits came so easy to me. In the back of my mind was also some guilt about having committed suicide in at least one past life in which I may have abandoned a family who loved and needed me. Edgar Cayce had said this guilt can be erased by patience and love, through forgiveness of one's self and others.

On Mondays and Tuesdays after work I rode the subway to Chinatown where the Literacy Center was located on the second floor of the library. After five weeks of training, I was assigned a small group of students. Some of the students were immigrants, and English was their second language. The majority was American and had graduated from high school, but somehow fell through the cracks without learning to read or write. Some were in their early twenties, a few were in their sixties. Two of my students, both in their early forties, had been drug addicts for twenty years. One man in his fifties, whose daughter had done all his writing for him, came to class so that he could keep track of his finances in his checkbook. One woman in her twenties knew the alphabet and simple words. She wanted to improve her vocabulary and be able to write letters. My fifth student looked liked a teen-ager. She had fled from mainland China with a friend during one night and now was newly married and had a child.

The program's way of teaching was unique. Each tutor, in charge of choosing the curriculum for her students, followed certain guidelines. We suggested that students pick their own books to read. A thirty-minute reading session was followed by a discussion or sharing period. Finally came the writing time when students wrote whatever they chose. While others read, I sat with each student for ten to fifteen minutes and gave feedback, making sure to praise at least one aspect and to recommend only one for improvement. I loved the opportunity to be creative in teaching my students. I brought in copies of a blank job application for practice, copies of Robert Frost's poem "The Wall," and Lincoln's Gettysburg Address.

Alex, one of my students, was a remarkable person. Shorter and not quite as tough looking as Charles Bronson, he was street smart. He was twice divorced and had four children. He thought the world of the woman he dated. For twenty years he had been addicted to hard drugs and alcohol. In his final years of addiction he lived on doorsteps and in cellar entrances on the Bowery. He told me that there was nothing between him and death except the thought of what his children would think of him if he died like a bum in the Bowery. That thought was worse than giving up drugs and alcohol. He went to Narcotics Anonymous (NA) and Alcoholics Anonymous (AA) and stayed clean. Within a short time of sharing his experiences and hopes at NA and AA meetings, group leaders discovered he was a good speaker who inspired others. Before he learned to read and write, he was invited to special anniversary meetings to tell his story—not only in New York, but also in other cities.

Alex wrote about the Twelve Steps of AA and NA programs. He did not let me read his writings, though, claiming they were too personal. I wondered, worried, and prayed about how I could help him improve if he continued to be secretive. After knowing me for a month, though, he trusted me and handed me his writings. He improved in a steady way, and his self-esteem rose along with his skills.

Twice a year the Literacy Center collected stories and poems from students and tutors to print in booklets. Most students wanted to have something they wrote included, if only two or three lines. It was something to be proud of. Alex wrote about a trip he took with his girlfriend along the west coast, and he took pride to spell correctly the names of the towns they passed through. When the booklet was printed, we had a "publishing party" with food and soda, and students and tutors stepped to the front and read their pieces to the group, followed by enthusiastic applause.

I made a commitment to stay for six months, but I stayed for almost two years. Giving two nights a week, plus time to study papers and work out a lesson plan, was draining. After two years it was time to move on, and there were others to take my place.

Recently I ran into Alex while standing in line to hear an inspirational speaker. He had earned his living as a welder six years before when I tutored him, but he was now working as a substance abuse counselor. He told me that he not only stayed clean, but had continued to improve his reading and writing skills.

Meanwhile, things were not going well for Brian in Florida. He could not find a job, and he seemed to be getting confused and paranoid. One night he called, exasperated. He wanted to move back to New York and get a job here, but no one would offer him a place to live. He said he would fly back to New York anyway and live on the streets.

I could not let that happen and invited him to stay with

me until he found a job and got back on his feet. Everyone, including myself, had been telling me it was a mistake. As it happened, I learned another valuable lesson regarding my fear of destructive masculine energy. After all, how could I learn to overcome fear? Certainly not by blindly running away each time I felt afraid. I had to face the fear and make the right decision about how to respond.

So, I bought an ice cream cake at the corner Häagen-Daas to welcome Brian. He ate the cake with appreciation, but he was not the same. He was depressed. In the following weeks he did little to find a job. When I came home from work at five-thirty, the blinds in the apartment were often still down and he had not gotten dressed. In the small space of my studio apartment we began to get on each other's nerves. Sometimes he went out for a walk, sometimes I did.

For me, it was a very painful and confusing time. It hurt me that he was so unhappy, had no energy, and was dispirited. I worried about him. The worst part was that he was looking for a victim to blame, and I was his victim. While he stayed at my apartment, I took a two-week trip to Germany that I had planned months before. I asked Brian to come with me to the airport, but he refused. No one had ever done that for him, and he would not do it for me. After the deep love we had shared, I felt hurt that he took such an attitude.

I visited my mother and brothers, my former schoolmates Christa and Rosemarie, my friend Monika, and my former roommates Erika and Sigrid. It was good to see them again, but I did not enjoy myself. I felt surrounded by an emotional darkness that I could not shake off. I worried about Brian. I worried about me. While at my mother's house, Brian called that he had found a job. We both rejoiced.

When I returned to New York, I expected a change for the better in Brian's attitude, but the reverse happened. His temper flared up constantly, especially on weekends when he had nothing to do but hang around the apartment. He was angry, and I was his convenient target. He began to verbally and viciously attack my metaphysical ideas and my Germanness.

Then he became physically violent, kicking his own suitcase and tearing up his own photographs. Next, he kicked a drawer in my beautiful wooden desk and then, intending to knock some of my books off the divider between the living room and kitchen, kicked a $300 microwave oven off the shelf behind the divider and broke it. "If I were six feet, like you, I'd kick your ass," I told him. I prayed. I meditated. I went with him to a session with a therapist. For me the issue was that he needed to control his anger while he stayed at my apartment, and I made that point with his therapist. She asked him to make a commitment to control his anger. In response, he angrily threw his wallet on the polished floor and let it crash. He was not willing to control his anger.

I discussed the situation with Mary, who was a counselor. (Frankie had left New York for another city.) I told her that the previous night Brian gave me the money he owed for rent and telephone, but he ripped it up and threw it in my face. "My mother was abusive," I complained to Mary, "and I just have not learned how to deal with abusive people."

Mary nearly laughed at what she perceived was my naivete. "You don't learn to deal with abusive people," she said firmly, "you get away from them!" She characterized Brian's behavior as "bizarre" and said, "It sounds as if he is what Alcoholics Anonymous people call a 'dry drunk.' " She also suggested that I visit a twelve-step group, such as Adult Children of Alcoholics. Even though there was no alcoholism in my family, she thought I might benefit from learning about addictive patterns of behavior.

Brian's behavior, unfortunately, did not improve. From reading feminist literature, I learned that men who verbally abuse women usually escalate into physical abuse. I knew that one of my lessons in this life and now in this relationship was to learn how to conduct myself when I was being abused and victimized. This was a moment of truth, a moment of facing myself. Who was I? I did not have a fear of physical abuse—I was utterly determined not to permit anyone to treat me with physical violence. But what about verbal violence? It left no visible scars. Other people need never know about it. I could deny it and pretend that I loved him and he loved me. But I could not pretend. I did not feel love nor did I feel loved. Over the years I had gone from repressing my feelings and escaping into my head to accepting and loving my feelings and recognizing they were an extension of my soul and were sacred. Brian was violating and abusing my feelings. He had destroyed the love I felt for him (I still felt love on a soul level), but I could not permit my feelings to be abused.

My love for him was not greater than my love for myself, and I demanded that he move out. I needed my safe space back. Now, I did not care if he ended up living on the street. On the physical level I could not love someone who endangered me. I remembered what I had learned from losing Franz-Heinz, as Aniya put into words: The connection of the heart does not insure continuance on the earth plane and, although separation is painful, it is a gift.

I spent the last week of his stay at a friend's apartment to be safe. I returned to my apartment and discovered that he had vacuumed and dusted. The money he owed me lay in the middle of the table. For several months after, he called frequently, apologized for his behavior, and asked how I was. He was more like his old self again, honest, matter of fact, did not blame, nor did he ask to come back. At this stage, the best I could do was to put him and his welfare into the hands of God. In His infinite love and wisdom, God would do the right thing for him.

After my experience with Brian, I had to take care of my feelings. I missed his physical presence very much, and I was afraid that he would die. I felt lonely, and I thought of how I felt when he touched me or when I touched him, when we lay in bed together. When I touched his body, I touched only goodness and love. I felt bliss when I touched him. Everything was all right when I touched him. His body was healthy, full of vitality, and fully alive.

I had told him that his thighs were every bit as handsome as Odysseus', and I meant it. I often told him that I was crazy about him, and I was. His body was the greatest body I ever touched. I thought his body was sacred. He had no feelings of embarrassment about it. He slept naked in winter and summer. He must have loved his body very much. I knew he loved my body. He often said that he loved my legs. I never thought my legs were great; they were short and strong. He often said that he loved my thighs, my waist, my breasts. When I walked naked through the room, he admired my body.

I remembered sleeping with him in many other beds at earlier times. Beds of leaves and grass in a depression in the ground in a dry, warm climate under the night sky full of glittering stars. We made love under God's open sky so many times that God knew us very well and knew also how much we loved each other. We were as physical and as playful with each other as puppy dogs.

If it were possible for people to have been animals, I would say that he and I had been mates in the animal kingdom, always snuggling up to each other, smelling each other, and delighting in each other. I wished we could have been animals together, just relating to each other with our bodies. We would have been happy together. But we were not animals but human beings, with minds, emotions, egos, and duties to ourselves: like going to work and getting an education and paying the rent and needing space and all that. Our bodies related to each other so well, happily, lustily, joyfully. Thanks, old friend. Thanks for the love you gave me. Thanks for every time you touched me.

Fully aware of my love for him, I needed next to look at my fear that he would die on the streets. When he moved out of my apartment, his father, whom he despised for his earlier alcoholism and his cruelty, put up the security and first month's rent. But knowing Brian's emotional and mental condition since he returned from Florida, I was not sure if he would keep either job or apartment. My fear for his survival was a daily presence in my mind.

It was an odd fear that I had not been aware of earlier. I thought that perhaps the fear was based on events many lifetimes before. Aniya had said we had been healers and mates in Eastern Europe, had fled and been pursued. He had been killed. Strangely, I could see pictures in my mind of a hilly country where everything was brown from too much sun: grasses, trees, bushes. I discussed my plan with Mary to do an "active imagination" exercise, in order to release whatever feelings caused the fear, and she encouraged me to do it.

So one evening, I prepared with spiritual reading and entered a meditative state. With candlelight and music by Vangelis, I retraced Brian's and my steps in my imagination, found his body, buried and mourned it. It was a very emotional exercise. The feeling that arose was extreme dependency on someone I loved as much as myself. When I finished, I went to sleep and awoke the next morning without the fear.

On my birthday in November, Brian came for a short visit to bring me a gift. He was vacating the apartment his father had paid rent on and moving in with a friend. I did not want to be alone with him, however, and met him in the lobby of my building. He opened the box he brought, and a sleepy six-month-old cappuccino-colored Siamese kitten with blue eyes looked up at me. She was gorgeous! I fell in love with her immediately, and she immediately accepted me. Brian had called her Billie, after "Billie" Holiday, but I called her Joya or Billie Joy. I thought of her symbolically as our "baby." I brought the kitty upstairs and accompanied Brian to a restaurant for a snack.

He apologized repeatedly for his previous abusive behavior. He said he had finally gotten back in touch with the church and with God, had made confession, and prayed regularly to Jesus to help him overcome his anger and his hatred. During the short time in the restaurant, he exploded angrily several times. I stayed detached, loving, no longer in an intimate relationship, loving him on another level, and in a public place I felt safe.

For several years I let my answering machine screen my calls and take messages, even if I was home—not to avoid calls from Brian—but calls from sales people. If he called during those years, he left no message. Later, I picked up calls as they came in and one was from Brian. I was glad to hear from him.

I asked about his life, and he said that he was excited because he was back in college at the City University of New York (CUNY) and taking courses in literature and drama. He asked about me and "our" cat. I told him we were both fine, and the cat was a delightful little pet. Brian made the same sound deep in his throat that he used to make when he was pleased or when he responded to and shared in my pleasure.

But he had karma to work out, and many lessons to learn about living on this planet. I hoped that the time we spent together had been of benefit to him, not on a superficial level, but on a soul level. I had loved him as well as I could. Making a commitment to love him had been for me a very enriching experience. It had lifted me completely out of my victim mode. When, at the end, the universe seemed to say,

"Well, now, let's see if you have really learned your lesson," and created circumstances in which I could have once again easily identified as victim, I simply said, "No more."

The universe also seemed to test me on a second lesson I'd been learning, namely forgiveness. Could I forgive Brian for his imperfections that led him to attempt to hurt me with cruel words? Because I was able to see that his cruelty came out of his own suffering, yes, I could forgive him completely.

Chapter 10
Victorious

> Not my will but Thine, O Lord, be done in and through me. Let me ever be a channel of blessings, today, now, to those that I contact, in every way. Let my going in, mine coming out be in accord with that Thou would have me do, and as the call comes, "Here am I, send me, use me."
>
> —(Edgar Cayce reading 262-3)

TOASTMASTERS, a national organization for people who want to give public speeches for fun, say that the number-one fear among Americans is the fear of speaking in public. Toastmasters offered a way to overcome this fear. I thought this was great and so, in December of 1987, I joined *Pacers,* a Toastmasters club with twenty members who met every other week in a conference room at the Mid-Manhattan Library on Fifth Avenue. I thought that if I consciously put myself in a situation that would provoke fear, I could work on overcoming it. To my utter surprise, my very first speech won the trophy for best speaker of the evening. This trophy was soon joined by a second, a third; later, an eighth and a ninth. A spiritual teacher, who knew about my fears and my need to develop confidence and self-esteem, once called my trophies "monuments to your conceit" and suggested that I trash them. "Real confidence does not come from trophies," he said, "but from what we think about ourselves on a day-to-day basis." Sometimes when I look at the shiny trophies on my bookcase, I say to myself, "There stand the monuments to my conceit," and I grin at the old teacher.

I gave many more speeches and used the opportunity to be creative and to take risks. The Club was a safe place to give speeches, and so I spoke about topics that had meaning to me: out-of-body experiences, why everyone should pay attention to their dreams, the drawing of mandalas, the seven chakras, and teaching literacy skills to adults.

From readings with Gloria and Aniya I knew that I had been a public speaker in two past lives: in ancient Rome, when my present-life father had been my teacher, and in Tibet. Both of these lives had been occasions of "flowering and opening up and of service," but in both lives that process had been brutally ended. The people in authority had become threatened by what I said about freedom and rights of the poor, slaves, and women. In Rome I had been thrown into prison, and in Tibet my tongue had been cut out. As I went about practicing and giving speeches, I was aware of the influences of these past-life experiences. I practiced more forgiveness and also used "reality talks" in that I would remind myself that those experiences lay in the past, that it was now safe to speak out, and could even be a pleasure.

Since I had left New York University in 1987, I had held three jobs in small organizations. While working at one of them, a publishing firm, the owner's daughter, Veronica, and her colleagues in the art department asked me to order their lunches. For some reason that I was not informed about, the person who previously sat at my work station had always ordered lunch for them. Veronica was not very nice about it; actually, she was quite rude. Could the artists not order their own lunches, I thought. I felt crazy with repressed anger, fear of authority, and guilt about my anger and was incapable of explaining rationally in the moment how I felt or what I was thinking. So, I ordered the lunches and then withdrew to a calm space to figure things out.

I took a couple of deep breaths and addressed my inner divinity, "God, my thoughts are crazy; give me Your thoughts." Then I listened. My mind was still. Suddenly a thought existed in the silence, "I wish they were all dead." I was shocked and stunned. Was that divinity speaking or was that my ego?

After five minutes, I asked again: "Father, my thoughts are crazy; give me Your thoughts." I waited in silence. Again, the response was, "I wish they were all dead." I remembered that in therapy with Peter early on, he wanted me to role-play my mother and speak threateningly, the way I had been spoken to by her. I resisted giving voice to the ugly threats I had been subjected to, but Peter told me that I had taken the ugliness of the threats into my psyche and that I could get rid of them by role playing. This was role playing, too. So this time, I allowed myself to wish them dead. Only their bodies could die; their souls were immortal. It was rather satisfying to imagine a world without the boss's daughter and her colleagues.

After another five minutes passed, I asked again and received the same response. I again pondered the message I had received, "I wish they were all dead." I certainly wasn't going to kill them. I wasn't even going to seriously wish them dead, nor did I wish them any harm at all. The image of children at play came into my mind. They often played at aggressively shooting people or running them over with a toy truck. They were not about to hurt anyone either, but their play at being aggressive served a purpose, I thought. It made them feel strong and created the sense that they were able to protect themselves. When I was a child, I had been punished for expressing anger and eventually been completely cut off from my natural instinct for self-protection.

When I asked the next time, "Father, my thoughts are crazy; give me Your thoughts," a new response came into my mind, namely, "And I blame no one." That thought certainly did not come from my ego. So, I could not blame Veronica for being rude and demanding, nor could I blame myself for wishing them dead. I was able to quickly let go of all blame, and as a result I felt wondrously free, centered, and even loving. I felt so sane and caring that I approached the owner and explained calmly how I felt about ordering lunch for the artists. He immediately understood my position and told his daughter they should take care of their own errands.

After leaving New York University, I had hoped to find a career path as a spiritual counselor, but that did not happen. Perhaps I was not ready to hold a professional post. God seemed to have other plans for me, and I bowed to His will. If He wanted me to be a secretary for the rest of my life, so be it.

In 1989 I realized that I had felt happier and safer in large organizations, such as the *Daily News* and New York University. One day I asked an acquaintance in my building, Ruth, who was a personnel manager at a multinational organization, if they were hiring new staff. She said yes and I applied. I took the test, and after that some things began to click.

On the evening after taking the tests, Ruth already knew that I had passed them and called me on the phone. She had spoken with a colleague of hers who needed an assistant. She had told him about me, including that I had graduated from NYU. He was about to travel to South America and said to her before he left, "She's from NYU? Hire her." I was hired on a three months' temporary basis, but was actually told the three-month period was the probationary time. It felt odd to me that I was not to meet the person I would work with, and I insisted on meeting with someone who could tell me about the position. My intuitive feeling, however, told me very strongly to accept the position.

In retrospect, this was the beginning of a very stressful time that lasted from April 1989 until about April 1992, when I completed my graduate studies. I am reminded of an Arcane School meditation, "The Burning Ground," in which the student invites God's divine burning fire to consume all that is negative within the personality in order to become a better server. Students were cautioned to work with this meditation only if they were ready go through the fire. In one form or another, I had offered myself and my life to God many times and was quite willing to walk once again on "the burning ground."

I had a beautiful working relationship with Carlos, my new boss. He had graduated from NYU and highly respected the university and its graduates. Since the corporation had many interests overseas, my first task was to write hundreds of letters requesting references on international candidates who had taken an examination and were being considered for positions in various parts of the world. When I brought him the first batch of letters, he said, surprised, "You've finished them already? You are giving the rest of us a bad name," and we both laughed.

After three months of working with him, I was pulled away by the director of the department to work with Mrs. Copper whose secretary was on extended leave. Mrs. Copper had retired at the age of sixty a few years ago and lived in Florida, but she was called back every summer to help out. She was a widow, gentle and soft-spoken, but strong. She had beautiful white hair, dark skin, and a slight Jamaican accent. I liked her gentleness and her steadiness. The fact that she had been a Unity student for twenty-five years put us on the same wavelength, and she soon invited me to call her by her first name, Beatrice.

The work in this position was specialized and more demanding. The grade of the position was two steps above the grade at which I had been hired. My predecessor had left several weeks earlier, and work was backed up. Being organized and conscientious, I took it upon myself to clear up the backlog and stayed several times a week for an extra hour or two. Months later I was told that the director had once remarked, "Jennifer cannot do the job in seven hours like the others; she needs nine hours." She had been unaware that there was a backup. If she had spoken to me about it, or if I had known about her remark earlier, I could have taken appropriate action.

After three months of working with Beatrice, I was pulled off that job and placed in another one across the hall in a small subdepartment where everyone seemed harried and short-tempered from overwork. The department head was about to retire and had emotionally withdrawn from the staff. Part of my daily job was to read hundreds of job applications and to direct them to the appropriate departments. For someone who knew the departments and their responsibilities, including branches in other countries, this would have been easy. As a newcomer to this huge organization, I found it was not easy. Still, I survived. Due to my experience in *Pacers*, I found communicating with my colleagues much easier than ever before and was able to get the information I needed. I made friends, baked cookies to cheer everyone up, and was declared "number-one baker." Eventually the head of the department retired and Celine, a young, married French woman with two children, took her place.

In the fall of 1989 I entered a graduate program in communications at the City University of New York at Hunter College. I wanted to study communication among people, even within people. I had little interest in media communication but was forced to take a number of courses in that area because Hunter did not have enough courses in human communication. Doing graduate school work after working at a demanding job is hard enough, but to take courses I did not like made it even more difficult.

During the summer of 1990 I learned that my job was in jeopardy. Celine, who liked me and my work, told me that the director, who also was in charge of this department, had told her, "Let's get rid of Jennifer. She is no good." Celine tried to tell her that my work was good and she liked me, but the director was unwilling to listen. During a phone conversation with Ruth, she remarked critically, without my prompting, that I had not "ingratiated" myself to the director. Truly, I thought, this is a strange world where people do strange things. I was not willing to "ingratiate" myself to the director, to behave toward her in such a way that betrayed my feelings. The director sounded like a rerun of my mother and one or two other authority figures in my past with whom I had been disappointed. How interesting, I thought, to get to do this again on a higher turn of the spiral of experience, until I get it right!

Fortunately, in the middle of the most intense stress, I was able to take a one-month vacation and spent three weeks of that time with Unity students. When I left New York for Missouri, it seemed that my job would come to an end on August 30. In my heart, I was convinced that I was doing a good job, and neither I nor God found any fault with me. Not only did I do a good job, but I was a more loving person than I had ever been in spite of trying circumstances. I had faith in the laws of the universe, and I was convinced of God's love for me and everyone. I had faith that whatever happened when I returned, it would be in my best interest. Meanwhile I would pray, meditate, and carry out God's will as best as I could. I was also determined to have a great time in the next three weeks and relax into God's love as much as I could.

Feeling calm and in touch with the peace in my soul, I

arrived at Unity Village, the headquarters of the Unity churches just outside Kansas City. Many of its red-brick buildings are reminiscent of medieval Italian monasteries, and the beautiful rose garden with its fountains and hidden among the buildings is an oasis outside time and space where one can easily connect to spiritual realities. During those two weeks several hundred students from all over the United States stayed in neat little cabins.

My roommate, Ellen, came from a family of German Lutherans in Minneapolis, and we immediately got along well. She registered for a course on grace, taught by Debbie Tyson, a teacher of metaphysics. We exchanged information on classes, and Ellen shared with me a prayer for healing that she learned in her class on grace. My own mental and emotional healing had progressed to the point where often I could no longer see what needed to be healed. I needed help, and this prayer put everything into the hands of God. He knew. He would bring to mind what needed my attention. I said the prayer with devotion that same night: "Father, into Thy hands I commit my spirit, my soul, and my body. Reveal all that needs to be revealed. Heal all that needs to be healed. Heal me in depth. Thy will be done. It is finished." It seemed such an innocuous little prayer, and after finishing it I wondered if it had reached God. I said it again, slower, with more devotion and more attention in pronouncing each word while focusing my mind intently on its meaning.

I awoke at midnight and watched a dream take place in my forehead, in that special place just between the eyebrows. I was at the beautiful grounds of Unity Village, and I saw about a dozen people on the grass beside the path. They were dancing, and all of them were on fire. Flames came out of their bodies, shooting up to above their heads, but no one got burned. No one got hurt. This was the kind of fire that did not burn and did not cause pain.

During a break the next morning, I approached Debbie Tyson, teacher of the class on grace, who also taught my class on metaphysics. I told her my dream, asking what it might mean. She had an instant recognition of its meaning. "Are you in my other class on grace?" she asked me.

"No," I said, "but my roommate is, and she taught me the prayer."

"So you've been saying it?" she asked.

"Yes," I answered.

"Well, that's it," she smiled. "The healing is happening. The fire is a healing fire. Even though you don't see yourself burning, it's really happening to you." I thanked her and walked away with a smile on my face, feeling joyous that God in me was active.

I consciously lived one day at a time. Every morning before breakfast I could be found in the little chapel for prayer and meditation. I prayed for myself, for the director's happiness, and blessed the organization of which I wanted to remain a part. The classes I took were interesting, Ellen was good company, and I met many other students from all over the U.S. I went for walks in the woods and swam in the Olympic-size swimming pool. I got on the plane for New York feeling refreshed and inspired.

After another week of raspberry picking and jam making, I returned to the office. I felt as if I were going through the "darkest hour before dawn," and I knew daylight had to come soon. Yes, it was scary. To counteract the anxiety, I renewed my dedication and conscientiousness while doing my work and intensified my spiritual practices. I thought that if I showed God how serious I was about doing His work, He must take care of me and give me a job where I could best use my abilities. If He wanted me to leave this organization, so be it, but my choice was to stay.

At the time I was a member in an A.R.E. Study Group and with other members became active in helping the homeless in New York. Sonja, Laura, Todd, and I would make sandwiches and take them to Grand Central Station and hand them out to hungry men and women there. On my own I frequently visited a shelter for homeless women and helped serve meals during dinner time. Keeping busy doing good work helped to stop me from worrying about losing my job. I wrote a short article about the experience of handing out sandwiches to homeless strangers, and it was published in *Venture Inward*, the magazine of the A.R.E. (July/August 1990) Tony, a handsome independent businessman, living in a city not far from New York, read the piece. He told me later that he instantly felt as if he knew me and contacted me. We became friends and eventually visited each other.

During the month of August, I had two interviews in other areas of the organization, one was arranged by Ruth, the other one by Celine. One post was in the legal department and offered long-term employment and immediate security, but required long sessions of legal dictation. The day after the interview, I was offered the position and long-term employment. The other post was in an international department and meant an initial short-term employment that could, however, be renewed and eventually become permanent. It also meant working with a colleague in my native language and having frequent contact with the government of my native country.

Pausing before the door behind which the second interview would take place, I felt a strong desire for this position. I asked for God's help to make the interview come out in my favor. Listening for an answer I felt, but almost heard, the words, "The decision has already been made." With the message came a feeling of calm. The following interview was a breeze, and two days later I was offered this position also.

Nearly all the people I asked to help me decide which position to accept urged me to take the one with the security. "The job market is tight," they said. Only one person, my friend Beatrice, an experienced and wise woman, said: "Follow your heart. The security will follow."

I followed my heart and accepted the position in the international department. My German boss, Günther, was a brilliant man and had a good sense of humor. He relied on me to edit and proofread his correspondence and reports and do translations from German into English. I had regular contact with members of the government in Bonn, and this contact let me examine once more the relationship with my roots and to heal remaining conflicts about being in a German body.

Since nothing happened by chance, there was a purpose for my birth and upbringing. I had addressed the issue of authority which misused its power, first in my relationship to my mother and finally with the director. I had made my repressed emotions conscious, released them, and used my mind to replace negative ones with positive ones. I had reeducated my desires and my personal will with the ideals work. I had also confronted and released my feelings of shame and unnecessary guilt. I could see clearly now that my self-image of insignificance and powerlessness had changed. I felt confident, competent, and effectual. I could not pretend that I had no psychological scars, but I no longer suffered; and if I suffered, I knew how to ask for help and let comforting people into my life. The old description of me, "Still waters run deep," was no longer true either. I could now talk privately and professionally to one person or to a group of people.

During this time I had a vivid dream about my mother, who had just announced her twelfth visit to the States. In the dream, I walked ahead of my mother on top of a mountain. It was an unusual mountain, as if it belonged to another dimension or as if it were God's mountain. There was something holy there. Above, I saw a huge tree, whose crown formed a design like two huge arms encircling a part of the sky. The tree grew above the mountain and yet it was below it. My mother climbed up the tree trunk and talked to me with sincerity and caring. She talked about me and what she felt about me. I only listened with half an ear but suddenly she got my full attention as she vehemently said, "But I would *not* take a chance and lose you!"

Had my physical mother changed and now loved me where she was indifferent before? Over the last thirty years I had seen her only intermittently when either one of us traveled across the ocean. After reflecting, I concluded that this dream had little to do with my biological mother, but more with the mother-in-me, that part of my psyche that mothered me. I believe that this dream describes that my feelings for me had been lifted to a higher level of consciousness. The mother-in-me, who originally disliked me as much as my biological mother did, responded to the divine love and caring that I had invited and now was an active loving force in my psyche. Would the changed inner relationship affect the outer relationship with my biological mother? Had I totally overcome my fear of my mother's powerful energy on the physical plane?

My mother visited New York in September 1991 for four weeks. I took a few vacation days and rode the bus to Newark airport, where I met Heinz and his wife Klara. When I thought about the two-and-a-half-hour ride to Heinz's house in the Catskills, I felt anxious and hoped I would not sit beside my mother in the back seat with no one else to talk to but her.

She arrived, a tiny old woman with gray hair and a strong face (she was now eighty-one years old). I greeted her with a hug. Sure enough, I sat beside her for two-and-a-half hours in the back seat, while my brother and his wife sat up front. But I was neither afraid nor angry. I was centered in myself and in my life, and I felt powerful. We talked during the entire trip. She told me what was going on in Germany with herself, my brothers, and other relatives.

She showed no interest in me or in my life and asked me no questions. In the past I took that as an indication that she was not interested and as a command not to speak about myself. But I had dropped that assumption. So, I told her about my work, my apartment, my friends, and the graduate work I was doing. She did not try to interrupt me, belittle me, nor did she pull any of her old tricks that used to make me feel manipulated, unloved, and powerless. I radiated my belief that I would not accept that nonsense. By fully owning, using, and focusing my own attention, she could not manipulate me. I felt beautiful. I thoroughly enjoyed the ride, her company, and my strength.

We arrived at my brother's house around 10:00 p.m. My mother was full of news, and we listened to her till midnight. Klara and I yawned and wanted to go to sleep. My mother, who was still on European time which was 6:00 a.m. already, showed no sign of tiredness. I appreciated her indefatigability and hoped I had inherited it and would have it when I reached the age of eighty-one.

My brother Heinz, who had the property, and I, who had the word-processing equipment, arranged our first family reunion, inviting ninety relatives on the Sunday after Labor Day. This reunion was a gift I made to my mother because I had forgiven and chose to be loving. We were blessed with incredibly beautiful weather, and temperatures reached the nineties. The mountains nearby radiated rich early autumn colors of gold and wine red in the leaves on the aspen and maple trees. My brother's lawn and the adjacent woods teemed with my brothers and sisters, cousins and their children, nieces, nephews, and several great nephews. Special guests were my mother and my father's sisters Anna and Wilhelmine, who had emigrated from Germany to the U.S.

in 1929 and 1935, but my mother was the matriarch and the "star" of the reunion, with seven children, fifteen grandchildren, and eight great-grandchildren to honor her.

The following year I graduated from CUNY with an M.A. degree in communications. I was the only immigrant member in my family with a college degree, and now I was also the only one with a master's degree. In my extended family, only one cousin had a master's degree, and my niece Linda received hers about the same time as I did. When friends ask me if I will go on to get my Ph.D., I shake my head and say with a smile, "Enough studying for now. Maybe later."

Shona has remained my friend, although since she got married I see less of her. She, her husband Rob, two other friends, and I got together in a restaurant recently to celebrate Rob's birthday. Shona brought a video camera, and we had fun performing for it. On the way home she became serious and mentioned that she was grateful to me for introducing her to metaphysics with my talk about reincarnation, karma, life after death, and angels. She said that if she had not known me, she would have suffered a great deal more over the sudden and violent death by shooting of her younger brother a few years ago. The possibility that he still existed in spirit after his body died had given her comfort, and the hope of reincarnation added meaning to his short life.

After we left the restaurant, we walked into the cold night through the snow that lay on Lexington Avenue and that still gently fell from the sky. We chatted about supposedly having been Native American twin sisters who supported each other in doing some of the things young braves did that were forbidden for squaws. Because of the falling snow, there was hardly any traffic. I stopped before crossing the avenue and pointed at the gorgeous bright full moon that hung over the city. "You know," I said, "wolves are actually doing a healthy thing for themselves when they howl at the moon."

Shona looked at me, grinned, and I could read her mind. She said, "Let's do it." So all five of us spread our feet and planted them firmly on the ground. We looked up at the moon, took a deep breath, and—howled. Then we looked at each other, laughed and giggled, and howled twice more.

Since Shona married in 1989, I was the only remaining member of the "double marriage club," a club which never had more than two members: she and I. I still had not given up on finding a partner, still prayed to God about it. Having turned my life over to Him so many times, I began to feel that my love life was out of my hands. There was a short relationship with Tony, and then there was Karl, Heinz's old hunting partner, who had become very wealthy.

Hanni had invited Karl, who was eighty-one years old, to a party at her house. I had not seen him for many years. His wife, Martha, had died two years before. In front of everyone, Karl asked me to marry him. He said, "You will never have to worry about money again, because I have plenty for both of us. I'll share everything I have with you. If you want to go to Florida, I'll take you there. If you want to travel around the world, I'll do that with you. I have a house by the ocean and a boat right outside the house. I'm alone, and I don't like it. I need somebody. Will you marry me?"

I knew Karl well and in particular remembered one summer holiday nearly thirty years earlier at Heinz's place in the Catskills. Tina, I, and some other people were down by the pond. I was feeling inconsolably sad that day and cried. Unlike my family who felt helpless when someone cried, Karl consoled me and made me feel better. Ever since then I had taken a liking to this man. He still looked handsome. This time it was my turn to console him. He was lonely, and he was afraid. I knew what that felt like. I sat beside him for some time and just talked and listened. I told him I felt honored that he wanted to marry me, but marrying a man of eighty-one was simply out of the question.

My M.A. degree made me a more qualified employee all around. I was also lucky; in spiritual terms, I received God's grace because my post in the international department was upgraded by two levels, a process set in motion before I arrived there. The upgrading was accompanied by a higher salary. Money accumulated in my account, and I decided to visit one of the places I longed to explore, either Peru, Egypt, or Greece. It just so happened that the A.R.E. planned a trip to Greece in 1993, and I signed up.

In May 1993 I traveled to Greece with an A.R.E. group of sixteen other people. This trip was beautifully planned by the A.R.E. and was a gift I gave myself for graduating from CUNY the year before. I would like to share two incidents that happened during the trip and which demonstrate to me how much I had grown. We had flown from New York to Athens on an Olympic airliner. On the plane I had sat next to Ellen Cayce, who is married to Greg Cayce, a grandson of Edgar Cayce. We had traveled by bus to Eleusis, Mycenea, and Epidaurus. Then we boarded the *Arcadia* and cruised among the Greek islands, visiting Mykonos, Rhodes, and then on to Patmos.

On Patmos we descended through a church into the cave in which St. John is supposed to have received The Revelation when he was100 years old. The cave was fit for a king; it had a view onto the blue Mediterranean. We saw the spot where St. John is supposed to have lain down and the piece of rock on the wall he gripped to raise himself. We took ten minutes to meditate. Leaning against the rock wall of the cave, I felt sad. I thought that for all individuals in the world to live in peace and harmony, as St. John had envisioned it, people must stop denying pain and feel it. Only then could they experience the joy to which they are heirs.

I was filled with compassion as I came out of the cave and stood in the shade of the kiosk near our bus and bought some post cards. When I finished the transaction, I looked around for the bus, and the wide street was completely empty. Had I made a mistake and the bus was up the hill around the bend? I rushed up the hill, feeling the hot Mediterranean sun on my head, only to see the road deserted. Here I was, abandoned and alone in a strange land. I felt anxiety in spite of a part of my mind stating calmly that I could have a taxi drive me the ten miles to the ship and reconnect to my tour there.

This was another opportunity to face my fear, I thought. I had learned in the past not to add guilt and shame to fear, nor despair and, most important, not to suffer in silence. So I breathed consciously and let myself feel the fear in my body. I remembered one spiritual teacher who had encouraged me to "let the old jaws flap," and I felt just a little bit giggly. Interestingly, my instinct to survive had kicked in and held all feelings in check. Next, I looked around for another human being who could keep me from feeling alone and abandoned—the Greek woman at the kiosk. "The bus has gone on without me," I cried to her, out of breath, "and left me behind."

She looked at me and never stopped smiling. "Ah," she said, "happens all the time. Not to worry. Here," she added, "have a cookie." She handed me a Greek cookie with pistachio nuts. She even spoke English and I could communicate with her. "No problem," she continued. "I call you a taxi, take you up to monastery. Meet your people there. Wait five minutes. Here, have some nice Greek coffee." She handed me a tiny cup with strong Greek coffee.

Within five minutes, a taxi arrived and I climbed in. The driver followed the route the bus had taken up the mountain. I was still tense, but I could not help enjoying the beautiful scenery, the winding road up the mountain, olive trees, and red blooming oleander bushes in their prime on either side. The fare was only 800 drachmas, about four dollars. The first person I saw was my roommate, Sally, and next to her was Ellen. I explained what had happened and received comforting hugs from both. Letting in their warmth broke the tension of the survival mode, and tears of relief ran down my face. Then we agreed on a better system to prevent such mishaps in the future.

The following night aboard the *Arcadia* with Sally sleeping in her bed, I woke up twice and retreated to the bathroom and wrote down two pages of dreams. During the dream-sharing meetings after breakfast on the following mornings, I was able to share pieces of them. What was most amazing about these dreams was that my energy had been transformed from victim to victor. In the final dream segment I was collecting debris but was halted by rain, an interruption which made me angry. I expressed the anger in a kind of dance, grunting, stamping my feet, and hitting the air with my fists. Not only was I in touch with my anger, but I used it neither against me nor against anyone else. The energy of my anger was transformed into power and joy. So, being left behind contained a lesson and was a blessing.

The second incident happened on the next to last day when we visited the Acropolis in Athens. Together with thousands of other visitors, I and my group climbed up the steps to the Parthenon, Athena's temple, at nine o'clock in the morning. There it stood on top of the highest hill in Athens—eight massive marble columns in front and back and seventeen on each side. I saw it with my eyes and felt it living inside my heart. As we walked up the final stairs, I breathed deeply and tuned in to my inner feelings. First, I heard little children playing and laughing, carefree children full of joy and happiness.

Suddenly, I saw and felt myself on these same stairs with other women on either side of me, before me, and in back of me. We wore long, flowing dresses, climbed up, and entered the temple. I saw myself among gentle and graceful women, going up and coming down the steps many times.

I had feelings of ethereal light and gracefulness. Leaving the group who listened to our English-speaking guide, Maria, as she explained and gave facts, I walked to the front of the Parthenon. I sat down on a rock to be alone with my feelings. Tourists were not allowed inside the temple, but strolled all around it, taking pictures or resting on a rock and sipping water. A small group of archaeology students could be seen inside the temple columns. Again I felt myself inside the temple and could feel the temple alive inside my heart, bursting it open with love, joy, and awe of the Divine.

I felt in awe here on the highest hill in Athens in front of Athena's temple. I felt love for spirit that lived in everyone and everything. I was at peace and very content. I felt my heart opening up to timeless spirit that permeated everything. Somewhere in my body there was excitement to be here again, to feel the spirit of this place once more. However, all too quickly the time passed. I met my fellow travelers at the bus, shared my impressions with Ellen, and asked Maria if small children had ever played a role in the ancient celebrations. She confirmed that they had.

As the bus rolled through Athens, Ellen informed us of our next destination. Then she said that several people had received interesting impressions at Athena's temple. She asked if I would come up front, take the microphone, and share my impressions with the group. I was still full of spirit, went up front, and took the microphone in my hand. Easily and gracefully I spoke into the mike as if I had done it many times before. I really felt healed.

I am proud of what I have accomplished so far in this life—an education, self-knowledge, and happiness. If it had not been for my out-of-body experiences and my past-life memories, the chances are very good that I would have committed suicide. If I had survived, I would probably have been bitter and discontent. I would still carry the fear of being victimized from past incarnations in my subconscious, and I would probably be a closed, uncommunicative, and boring woman. I would not be in touch with my feelings nor in touch with the Divine that flows through me and everyone.

When I arrived in the U.S. in 1961, I felt guilty, ashamed, powerless, insignificant, and that I was everybody's scapegoat and victim. I was not in touch with my power or my will. Now my life is in the hands of God. I trust in God's love and wisdom. I am a channel for His will. God's will is my will, and God's power is my power. I am where I am today because of God's grace. I feel at peace with myself; I am creative and content.

I finally see my psychic sensitivity no longer as a liability but as an asset. Where I used to see only myself as the problem in relationships, now I am often the solution. Even with people who misuse their power, I am quicker to see what is going on, can pull myself out of the victim position, and ask God, "Now, how can I help this person?"

I still practice forgiveness whenever I think that someone has hurt me or when I remember an old hurt from the past. Old emotional scars, like physical ones, can keep on hurting just because the weather has changed. I combine forgiveness with prayer and contemplation.

I have mixed feelings about being single, largely because society and my family stamp a single person as a second-class citizen. Yet I am also certain that my singleness is karmic. Perhaps it is the result of my past suicide, while I was married. I am certain, however, that the experiences of marriage and children would have prevented me from freeing myself from the deep psychological conflicts that I worked through in this lifetime. Because of my singleness, I achieved self-knowledge, education, and happiness.

I still look and feel young and certainly am not too old to marry. I know of women who married for the first time in their sixties. There are men in my life today with whom I have caring relationships. Intuitively I feel that marriage lies ahead. When and if I marry, it will not be to fulfill society's expectation of me, but because I love someone, feel loved by him, and because I want to enter into a marriage relationship that has the ideal of spiritual growth for both partners.

The image of the nine-headed hydra and the kneeling Hercules is still meaningful to me. I must be humble before I can admit that I hurt or am afraid. To stop the fearful thought by cutting off the hydra's head is not enough. I will continue to get to the bottom of my fear, whether it originated in childhood or in a past life, and humbly lift the whole complex into the light of consciousness. This work will probably continue for as long as I live. As I continue to face myself, my weaknesses and my strengths, honestly and fearlessly, I believe I am performing a difficult but rewarding labor, just like Hercules, the universal disciple. Facing myself truly empowers me.

FOR FURTHER READING

Alcyone. *At the Feet of the Master.* The Theosophical Publishing House, Wheaton, Ill., 1984.

Atwater, Phyllis. *Coming Back to Life: The Aftereffects of the Near-Death Experience.* Ballantine Books, New York, N.Y., 1989.

Atwater, Phyllis. *The Magical Language of Runes.* Bear & Co., Santa Fe, N.M., 1990.

Bailey, Alice A. *Discipleship in the New Age, Vol. I.* Lucis Trust Publishing Co., New York, N.Y., 1944.

Bailey, Alice A. *Esoteric Psychology, Vol. I.* Lucis Trust Publishing Co., New York, N.Y., 1962.

Bailey, Alice A. *A Treatise on Cosmic Fire.* Lucis Trust Publishing Company, New York, N.Y., 1962.

Casriel, Daniel. *A Scream Away from Happiness.* Grosset and Dunlap, New York, N.Y., 1972.

Cayce, Hugh Lynn. *Faces of Fear.* Berkley Books, New York, N.Y., 1980.

Cerminara, Gina. *Many Mansions.* William Sloan Associates, New York, N.Y., 1950.

Church, W.H. *Many Happy Returns: The Lives of Edgar Cayce.* Harper & Row, San Francisco, Calif., 1984.

Evans, Patricia. *The Verbally Abusive Relationship.* Bob Adams, Inc., Holbrook, Mass., 1992.

Ferrucci, Piero. *What We May Be.* J.P. Tarcher, Los Angeles, Calif., 1982.

Furst, Jeffrey. *Edgar Cayce's Story of Attitudes and Emotions.* A.R.E. Press, Virginia Beach, Va., 1972.

Gaskell, G.A. *Dictionary of All Scriptures and Myths.* The Julian Press, New York, N.Y., 1960.

Giraudoux, Jean. "Ondine." From *Contemporary Drama: 13 Plays.* Selected and edited by Stanley Clayes and David Spencer. Charles Scribner's Sons, New York, N.Y., 1970.

Head, Joseph, and Cranston, S.L. *Reincarnation in World Thought.* Julian Press, New York, N.Y., 1967.

Hodson, Geoffrey. *The Coming of the Angels.* Rider & Co., London, Eng., 1932.

Karpinski, Gloria. *Where Two Worlds Touch.* Ballantine Books, New York, N.Y., 1990.

Keyes, Elizabeth Laurel. *Toning.* DeVorss & Co., Marina del Rey, Calif., 1973.

Kübler-Ross, Elisabeth. *On Death and Dying.* Macmillan Publishing Co., New York, N.Y., 1969.

Langley, Noel. *Edgar Cayce on Reincarnation.* Paperback Library, Inc., New York, N.Y., 1967.

Maclean, Dorothy. *To Hear the Angels Sing.* Lorian Press, Elgin, Ill., 1980.

McPherson, Sigrid R. *The Refiner's Fire: Memoirs of a German Girlhood.* Inner City Books, Toronto, Canada, 1992.

Metroux, Alfred. *History of the Incas.* Schocken Books, New York, N.Y., 1969.

Miller, Alice. *The Drama of the Gifted Child.* Basic Books, New York, N.Y., 1981.

Moody, Raymond. *Life After Life.* Bantam Books, New York, N.Y., 1975.

Muldoon, Sylvan. *The Case for Astral Projection.* The Aries Press, Chicago, Ill., 1936.

Muldoon, Sylvan, and Carrington, Hereward. *The Phenomenon of Astral Projection,* Rider and Co., United Kingdom, 1951.

Muldoon, Sylvan, and Carrington, Hereward. *The Projection of the Astral Body.* Samuel Weiser, New York, N.Y., 1970.

Müller, Max. *Three Lectures on the Vedanta Philosophy.* Longman, Green and Co., London, Eng., 1894.

Newhouse, Flower A. *Rediscovering the Angels.* The Christward Ministry, Escondido, Calif., 1950.

Pagels, Elaine. *The Gnostic Gospels.* Vintage Books, New York, N.Y., 1979.

Rilke, Rainer Maria. "The Tenth Elegy." *The Selected Poetry of Rainer Maria Rilke.* Vintage Books International, New York, N.Y., 1982.

Rodegast, Pat. *Emmanuel's Book II.* Bantam Books, New York, N.Y., 1989.

Roerich, Helene. *Mother of the World.* Agni Yoga Society, New York, N.Y., 1956.

A Search for God, Books I and II. A.R.E. Press, Virginia Beach, Va., 1990.

Schierse-Leonard, Linda. *The Wounded Woman.* Shambhala Books, London and New York, 1985.

Sechrist, Elsie. *Death Does Not Part Us.* A.R.E. Press, Virginia Beach, Va., 1992.

Sechrist, Elsie. *Dreams, Your Magic Mirror.* Cowles Education Corporation, New York, N.Y., 1968.

Steiner, Claude. *Scripts People Live.* Bantam Books, New York, N.Y., 1975.

Stevenson, Ian. *Twenty Cases Suggestive of Reincarnation.*

University Press of Virginia, Charlottesville, Va., 1974.

Sugrue, Thomas. *There Is a River.* Holt, Rinehart and Winston, New York, N.Y., 1942.

Von Franz, Marie Louise. *The Feminine in Fairytales.* Spring Publications, Dallas, Tex., 1972.

Weiss, Brian L. *Many Lives, Many Masters.* Simon & Schuster, New York, N.Y., 1988.

Woodman, Marion. *Addiction to Perfection.* Inner City Books, Toronto, Canada, 1982.

Woodman, Marion. *The Pregnant Virgin.* Inner City Books, Toronto, Canada, 1985.

Woodward, Mary Ann. *Be Still and Know.* A.R.E. Press, Virginia Beach, Va., 1962.

Woolger, Roger. "Jungian Past-Life Therapy." Tape #A 182. Sounds True Recording, 735 Walnut Street, Boulder, CO 80302.

Woolger, Roger. *Other Lives, Other Selves.* Bantam Books, New York, N.Y., 1987.

World Mythology. Chartwell Books, Secaucus, N.J., 1965.

Wright, Machaelle Small. *Behaving as if the God in All Life Mattered.* Perelandra, Jeffersonton, Va., 1987.

About the Author

Jennifer Borchers was born in Germany and emigrated to the United States as a teen-ager in 1961. Obtaining her U.S. citizenship five years later, she went on to receive a bachelor's degree in liberal arts from New York University and a master's degree in communication from the City University of New York at Hunter. Presently she is a member of the staff of the United Nations Board of Auditors.

A longtime member of the Association for Research and Enlightenment, Inc., she has also studied with the Arcane School, a metaphysical correspondence school, and is a former Toastmaster. Ms. Borchers also works as a public relations officer for the U.N. Staff Recreation Council's Society for Enlightenment and Transformation. Her writings on spiritual topics have appeared in *The Waterways Poetry Project*, *Spirit Guide*, *The Open Door*, and *Venture Inward* magazine. She lives in New York City with her Siamese cat, Billie Joy.

What Is A.R.E.?

The Association for Research and Enlightenment, Inc. (A.R.E.®), is the international headquarters for the work of Edgar Cayce (1877-1945), who is considered the best-documented psychic of the twentieth century. Founded in 1931, the A.R.E. consists of a community of people from all walks of life and spiritual traditions, who have found meaningful and life-transformative insights from the readings of Edgar Cayce.

Although A.R.E. headquarters is located in Virginia Beach, Virginia—where visitors are always welcome—the A.R.E. community is a global network of individuals who offer conferences, educational activities, and fellowship around the world. People of every age are invited to participate in programs that focus on such topics as holistic health, dreams, reincarnation, ESP, the power of the mind, meditation, and personal spirituality.

In addition to study groups and various activities, the A.R.E. offers membership benefits and services, a bimonthly magazine, a newsletter, extracts from the Cayce readings, conferences, international tours, a massage school curriculum, an impressive volunteer network, a retreat-type camp for children and adults, and A.R.E. contacts around the world. A.R.E. also maintains an affiliation with Atlantic University, which offers a master's degree program in Transpersonal Studies.

For additional information about A.R.E. activities hosted near you, please contact:

A.R.E.
67th St. and Atlantic Ave.
P.O. Box 595
Virginia Beach, VA 23451-0595
(804) 428-3588

A.R.E. Press

A.R.E. Press is a publisher and distributor of books, audiotapes, and videos that offer guidance for a more fulfilling life. Our products are based on, or are compatible with, the concepts in the psychic readings of Edgar Cayce.

We especially seek to create products which carry forward the inspirational story of individuals who have made practical application of the Cayce legacy.

For a free catalog, please write to A.R.E. Press at the address below or call toll free 1-800-723-1112. For any other information, please call 804-428-3588.

A.R.E. Press
Sixty-Eighth & Atlantic Avenue
P.O. Box 656
Virginia Beach, VA 23451-0656